DISCARDED

# WHERE DO BABIES COME FROM?

## Susan Meredith

### Designed by Lindy Dark

### Illustrated by Sue Stitt and Kuo Kang Chen

Consultants: Dr Kevan Thorley
and Cynthia Beverton of Relate, Marriage Guidance Council

j
QP251
m4
1991

## CONTENTS

| | | | |
|---|---|---|---|
| All about babies | 2 | Newborn babies | 14 |
| Starting to grow | 4 | What makes a baby like it is? | 16 |
| What is it like being pregnant? | 6 | What do babies need? | 18 |
| Mothers and fathers | 8 | A new baby in the family | 20 |
| How does a baby start? | 10 | Babies in nature | 22 |
| How is a baby born? | 12 | Index | 24 |

# All about babies

As the baby grows, its mother's tummy gets bigger.

Everybody who has ever lived was once a baby and grew in their mother's tummy. This book tells the story of how babies come into the world and begin to grow up.

A baby grows in a sort of hollow bag called the womb or uterus. This is a warm, safe place for it to be until it is big and strong enough to survive in the outside world.

## Food and oxygen

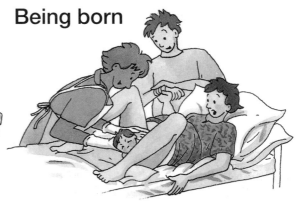

An unborn baby shares its mother's food and oxygen.

## Being born

The baby needs food to stay alive and grow. It also needs oxygen from the air. But babies cannot eat or breathe in the womb. They get food and oxygen from their mother's blood.

The baby stays inside its mother for about nine months. That is about 38 weeks. Then it is ready to be born. It gets out of its mother's tummy through an opening between her legs.

## Feeding

At first the only food a baby needs is milk, either from her mother's breasts or from feeding bottles. She needs to be fed every few hours.

## Crying

It is not always easy to figure out what a baby's crying means.

A newborn baby can do nothing for herself, so she requires a lot of attention. Crying is her only way of telling people she needs something.

## Baby animals

A cow's tummy gets fatter as her calf grows inside her.

Kittens feed on milk from their mother's nipples.

Many animals grow in their mothers' tummies and are born in the same way as people. They also get milk from their mothers.

## Growing up

Babies gradually learn to do more and more for themselves.

Many animals separate from their parents when they are very young. It is years before children can manage without their parents' help.

3

# Starting to grow

Everybody is made of millions of tiny living bits called cells. A baby starts to grow from just two very special cells, one from its mother and one from its father. Together, these two cells make one new cell.

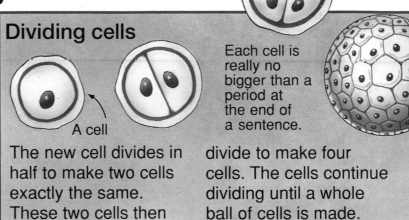

## Dividing cells

A cell

The new cell divides in half to make two cells exactly the same. These two cells then divide to make four cells. The cells continue dividing until a whole ball of cells is made.

Each cell is really no bigger than a period at the end of a sentence.

## In the womb

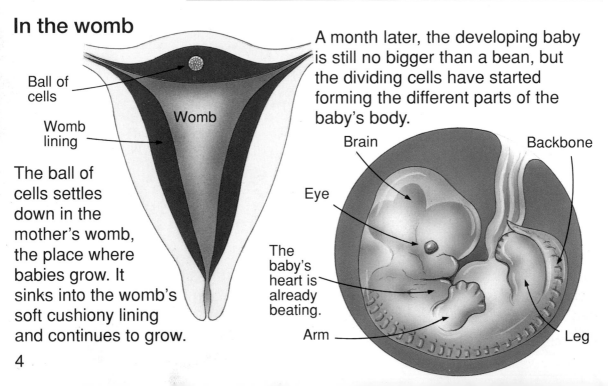

Ball of cells

Womb lining

Womb

The ball of cells settles down in the mother's womb, the place where babies grow. It sinks into the womb's soft cushiony lining and continues to grow.

A month later, the developing baby is still no bigger than a bean, but the dividing cells have started forming the different parts of the baby's body.

Brain

Backbone

Eye

The baby's heart is already beating.

Arm

Leg

## The baby's lifeline

The baby is attached to the lining of the womb by a special cord. The food and oxygen the baby needs go from its mother's blood down the cord and into the baby's body.

Like everybody else, the baby needs to get rid of waste. This goes down the cord from the baby's blood into its mother's blood. Her body gets rid of it when she goes to the toilet.

This is called the placenta. It grows on the lining of the womb.

Blood vessels

The cord is called the umbilical cord.

The placenta is where food, oxygen and waste pass between the mother's blood and the baby's.

The baby floats in a bag of special water. This acts as a cushion and protects the baby from harm.

The baby cannot drown in the water because it does not need to breathe until it is born.

## Getting bigger

The baby continues to grow. It moves and kicks, and also sleeps. It can hear its mother's heart beating and noises from outside her body too. Some babies even get hiccups.

Eventually, most babies settle into an upside-down position in the womb.

Some babies suck their thumbs.

5

# What is it like being pregnant?

When a mother has a baby growing inside her, it is called being pregnant. While she is pregnant, her body changes in all sorts of ways.

## Check-ups

The mother has regular check-ups to make sure she and the baby are healthy. These are given by a midwife or doctor. A midwife is someone who looks after pregnant mothers.

The mother is weighed. She should put on weight as the baby grows.

The mother's blood and urine are tested. This tells the doctor if the mother and baby are well.

## Looking after herself

The mother has to take special care of herself. If she is well, the baby is more likely to be healthy too.

It is not good for the baby if the mother smokes, drinks alcohol or takes certain medicines.

She is feeding her baby as well as herself, so she has to eat healthy food.

The mother's body has to work harder than usual, giving the baby what it needs. She has to rest more.

Gentle exercise pumps more blood through to the baby and makes the mother feel better too.

When the mother's tummy gets big, she should not carry heavy things. She may strain her back.

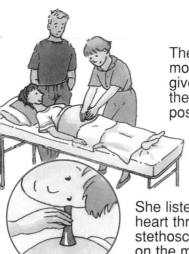

The doctor feels the mother's tummy. This gives her an idea of the baby's size and position.

She listens to the baby's heart through a special stethoscope. She puts it on the mother's tummy.

## Photos of the baby

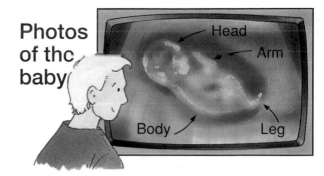

Head
Arm
Body
Leg

A machine called an ultrasound scanner takes moving pictures of the baby in the womb. These appear on a television screen and show everyone how the baby is developing.

## Kicking

After about five months, the mother feels the baby moving. Later, it will kick.

You may feel the kicks if you put your hand on the mother's tummy.

Eventually the mother can see her tummy moving and even guess whether a bump is a hand or a foot.

## Getting bigger

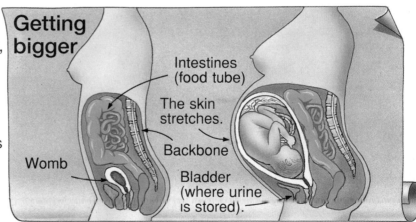

Intestines (food tube)

The skin stretches.

Backbone

Womb

Bladder (where urine is stored).

The mother's womb is normally the size of a small pear. As the baby grows, the womb stretches and other things in her body get squashed up. This can be a bit uncomfortable but everything goes back to normal later.

# Mothers and fathers

The special cells from the mother and father which make a baby start to grow are the sex cells. They are different from each other.

## Egg cells

The mother's sex cell is called an egg cell or ovum. She has lots of egg cells stored in her body, near her womb.

Tube

Egg

Ovary

Womb lining

Womb

Tube

Ovary

The egg cells are stored in the mother's two ovaries.

Once a month, an egg cell travels from one of the ovaries down one of the tubes leading to the womb.

Every month the lining of the womb gets thick and soft with blood. It is getting ready for a baby to start growing there.

There is a stretchy tube leading from the womb to the outside of the mother's body. It is called the vagina.

Babies are born through the opening of the vagina, which is between the mother's legs.

Vagina

The vaginal opening is quite separate from the ones for going to the toilet. It is between the two, just behind the one for urine.

This picture shows where the mother's baby-making parts are located.

8

## Sperm

The father's sex cell is called a sperm cell. Sperm are made in the father's two testicles. The testicles are in the bag of skin which hangs behind his penis

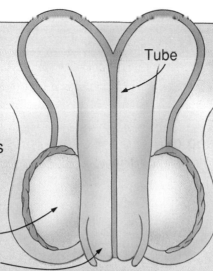

Tube

Testicle

Penis

The father's baby-making parts are between his legs.

Sperm can travel from the testicles along two tubes and out of the end of the penis.

Urine never comes out of the penis at the same time as sperm.

## Growing up

Young girls and boys cannot become mothers and fathers. Your baby-making parts do not start working properly until the time when your body starts to look like a grown-up's.

## What if a baby doesn't start?

If a baby does not start to grow, the womb's thick lining is not needed. The lining and the egg cell break up and trickle out of the mother's vagina with some blood.

This takes a few days each month and is called having a period. To soak up what comes out, the mother puts things called tampons in her vagina or places pads in her panties.

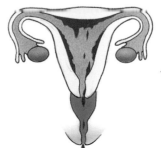

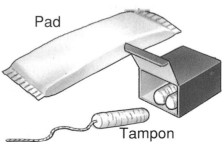

Pad

Tampon

9

# How does a baby start?

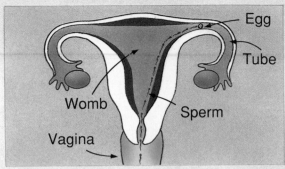

A baby starts to grow when an egg and sperm meet and join together. They do this inside the mother's body. The way the sperm get to the egg is through the mother's vagina.

Sperm cells come out of the opening at the end of the penis and swim up into the mother's womb and tubes. If the sperm meet an egg in the tubes, one of them may join with it.

The mother and father cuddle each other very close. The father's penis gets stiffer and fits comfortably inside the mother's vagina. This is called making love or having sex.

Sperm have long tails which they flick. This helps them to swim.

The moment when the egg and sperm join together is called conception or fertilization. Now a baby can start to grow.

10

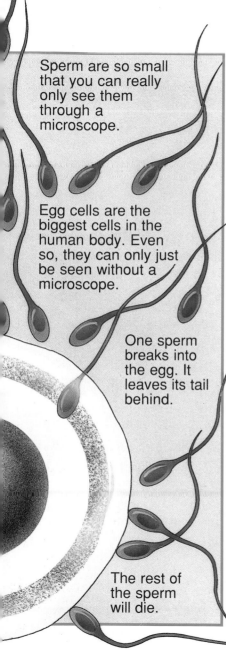

Sperm are so small that you can really only see them through a microscope.

Egg cells are the biggest cells in the human body. Even so, they can only just be seen without a microscope.

One sperm breaks into the egg. It leaves its tail behind.

The rest of the sperm will die.

# Pregnant or not?

It is several months before the mother's tummy starts to get

Calendar

bigger but she has other ways of knowing she is pregnant.

If she is pregnant, her monthly periods stop. The lining of the womb is needed for the growing baby.

Some pregnant mothers feel sick. This is caused by chemicals called hormones in their blood.

The hormones may make the mother dislike foods she usually likes or they may make her crave some foods.

Her breasts get bigger and may feel a bit sore. They are getting ready to make milk when the baby is born.

To be sure she is pregnant, the mother's urine is tested to see if it has one of the pregnancy hormones in it.

# How is a baby born?

After nine months inside its mother, the baby is ready to be born. It has to leave the warm, safe womb and move down the vagina to the outside world. This is called labor, which means hard work.

## Labor

The womb is really a very strong muscle. During labor, it keeps on squeezing and squeezing until the baby comes out of it. Each squeeze is called a contraction.

The baby will not need its placenta for much longer.

The mother's other leg has been left out of this picture so you can see the baby clearly.

The vagina stretches easily to let the baby pass through. Afterwards it goes back to its normal size.

The contractions pull the womb open and squeeze the baby through the opening.

Vagina

Placenta

During labor, the bag of water around the baby bursts. The water drains away out of the mother's vagina.

Towards the end of labor, the mother pushes hard to help the baby out. Soon after the baby is born, the placenta and empty water bag come out of the vagina too.

## When does labor start?

When the baby is ready to be born, special hormones are made in its blood. These go down the umbilical cord to the mother's body and make the contractions start.

The mother feels the contractions as pains in her tummy.

Most mothers go to hospital to have their baby. Some choose to have theirs at home.

12

# Helping the mother

Having a baby is exciting but can be exhausting and take many hours. A doctor looks after the mother during labor. The father can help too.

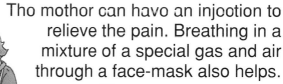

The father might rub the mother's back if it aches, or encourage her to relax and breathe properly.

The mother can have an injection to relieve the pain. Breathing in a mixture of a special gas and air through a face-mask also helps.

## The baby's heartbeat

The doctor listens to the baby's heartbeat during labor to make sure it is all right. In hospitals, the heartbeat is sometimes measured by a machine called a monitor.

The monitor is connected up to the mother's tummy.

Monitor

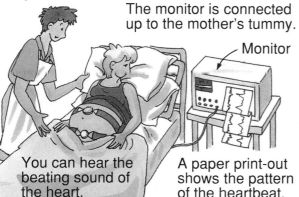

You can hear the beating sound of the heart.

A paper print-out shows the pattern of the heartbeat.

## What is a Caesarian birth?

Sometimes the baby cannot be born in the usual way. Instead it is lifted out through a cut in the mother's tummy. This is called a Caesarian.

The mother has a pain-killing injection so she cannot feel what is going on.

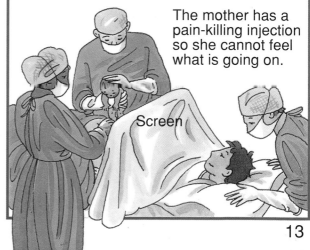

Screen

# Newborn babies

The first thing everyone does as soon as a baby is born is to look between its legs. Is it a girl or a boy?

The doctor checks that there is no liquid in the baby's nose or mouth. Now he can start to breathe.

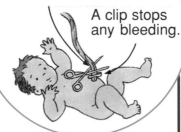

The cord is cut here. The baby cannot feel it.

A clip stops any bleeding.

Now that the baby can eat and breathe on his own, he no longer needs his umbilical cord. It is cut off.

Clip

The tiny bit of cord that is left dries up and falls off in a few days. Your tummy button is where your cord was.

The doctor checks that the baby is well and weighs him. He will be weighed often to make sure he is growing.

In the hospital, a newborn baby has a name label put on his wrist. This avoids any mix-up about whose baby he is.

Name label

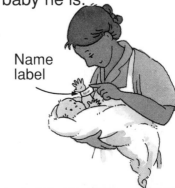

# Getting used to the world

The baby has been safe and comfortable in the womb for nine months. It is probably quite a shock to find herself in the outside world. She may also be tired from the birth.

The baby will get used to her new surroundings better if she is held and spoken to very gently. It may also help if things are kept fairly quiet and dimly lit at first.

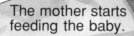
The mother starts feeding the baby.

The parents cuddle the baby and start getting to know her. Sisters and brothers come to meet her.

Newborn babies have to be wrapped up warm. Their bodies lose heat quickly.

Some newborn babies are almost bald. Others have a lot of hair. Some have hair on their body too. This soon rubs off.

Babies have a soft spot on their head. Bones gradually grow over it but until then it has to be protected.

Babies born in hospital usually sleep in a see-through cot by their mother's bed.

At first, babies all have blue eyes. The color may gradually change.

## Incubators

If a baby is very small or unwell when she is born, she may have to go in an incubator for a while. This is a see-through cot which is all enclosed and very warm.

The parents can touch the baby through windows in the incubator.

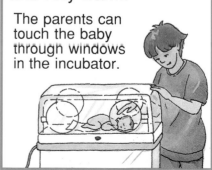

15

# What makes a baby like it is?

The mother's egg and the father's sperm cell together have all the instructions needed for a baby to grow in the way it does.

## Chromosomes

The instructions are carried on special threads in the cells. The threads are called chromosomes. The proper word for the instructions is genes.

This picture shows part of a chromosome.

The instructions are in a complicated code a bit like a computer program.

When the egg and sperm join together at conception, the new cell gets the chromosomes from both of them. Copies of these are passed to every cell in the baby's body.

The baby's cells have 46 chromosomes each, 23 from the egg and 23 from the sperm.

Because you have chromosomes from both your parents, you will take after both of them. The mixture of the two sets of instructions also means that you are unique.

Some things about you, like the way you look, depend a lot on your chromosomes. Other things depend as well on the type of life you have after you are born.

You are more likely to become a good swimmer if you are taken to the swimming pool a lot.

# Girl or boy?

Whether a baby is to be a girl or a boy is settled at conception. It depends on one chromosome in the egg and one in the sperm. These are the sex chromosomes.

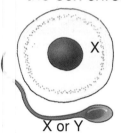

X or Y

The sex chromosome in all egg cells is called X. Half the sperm also have an X sex chromosome but half have one called Y.

If a sperm with an X chromosome joins with the egg, the baby is a girl.

Girls have two X sex chromosomes.

XX

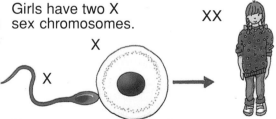

X

X

If a sperm with a Y chromosome joins with the egg, the baby is a boy.

Boys have one X and one Y sex chromosome.

XY

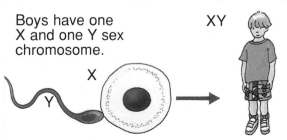

X

Y

# Twins

Twins grow in their mother's womb together and are born at the same time, one by one. A few twins are identical, which means exactly alike. Most twins are non-identical, which means not exactly alike.

Sometimes, when the new cell made at conception splits in two, each half grows into a separate baby. These twins are identical because they come from the same egg and sperm.

Identical twins are always the same sex.

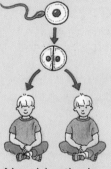

Sometimes, two separate sperm meet and join with two different eggs at the same time, and two babies grow. These twins are not identical because they come from different eggs and sperm.

Non-identical twins may be the same sex or one of each sex.

17

# What do babies need?

Babies need to have everything done for them. They have to be fed and kept warm, comfortable and clean.

They need lots of love and attention, and they need interesting things going on around them.

## Breast-feeding

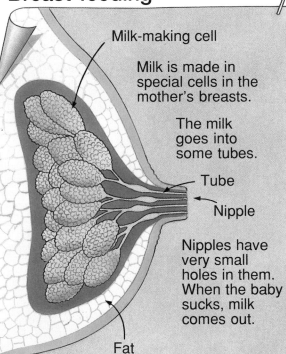

Milk-making cell

Milk is made in special cells in the mother's breasts.

The milk goes into some tubes.

Tube

Nipple

Nipples have very small holes in them. When the baby sucks, milk comes out.

Fat

When a mother has a baby, milk starts being made in her breasts. Hormones in her blood make this happen. Whenever the baby sucks at the breast, more milk is made.

If a mother is breast-feeding, she needs to eat well, drink plenty and get extra rest.

Breast milk is made from substances in the mother's blood and is the best food for a baby. It has chemicals called antibodies in it. These help the baby to fight off illnesses.

## Bottle-feeding

If babies are not being breast-fed, they have special powdered milk instead. This is usually made from cow's milk but is then altered to make it more like breast milk.

Special powdered milk is mixed with water for a baby's bottle.

Ordinary cow's milk is too strong for babies.

# Cuddles

A young baby's neck is not strong enough to hold her head up. Her head needs something to rest on all the time.

A cushion will keep your arm from aching.

Babies need a lot of cuddles to make them feel safe and contented. They need to be handled gently though.

Babies cannot fight off germs like older people, so their bottles have to be especially clean. This is done by sterilizing, which means getting rid of germs.

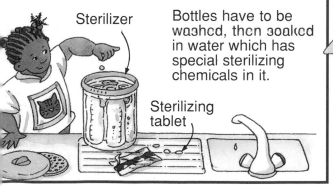

Sterilizer

Bottles have to be washed, then soaked in water which has special sterilizing chemicals in it.

Sterilizing tablet

# Diapers

A young baby may need as many as eight diaper-changes in a day.

If a wet or dirty diaper is not changed, the baby is more likely to get a diaper rash.

Babies do not know in advance that they need to go to the toilet. They only learn to tell as they get older.

# Sleeping

Babies have no idea of day and night at first.

It can take them a long time to learn to sleep through the night.

Some young babies sleep for as many as 18 hours a day. They wake up every few hours to eat though, even in the night. Nobody knows why some babies sleep more than others.

# A new baby in the family

This is an exciting, enjoyable time but it is also hard work. And it can take a while to get used to having a brand-new person in the family.

A new baby takes up so much of her parents' time and attention that older brothers and sisters can even feel a bit jealous at first.

## The mother's body

It takes a few weeks for the mother's body to go back to normal after having the baby, and she needs to rest. Both parents will be tired from getting up in the night to the baby.

## Helping

You could gather things that are needed for the baby and put them away.

It is useful for the parents to have help around the house at first. As the baby gets older, you could help by, for example, giving her a bottle.

## Crying

A baby's crying is hard to ignore. This is useful for the baby: it makes people look after him. Babies cry for various reasons. Nobody really knows why some cry more than others.

Is the baby hungry? Is he uncomfortable or in pain? Is he too hot or too cold, bored, tired, lonely or frightened?

Babies cannot wait for things. They have not learned to think about other people's feelings and if they do have to wait long, for something like food, they may even become ill.

Brothers and sisters can sometimes feel left out.

# Playing with a baby

A new baby will not be able to play with you for some time but she may soon start to enjoy watching you play nearby. Once you start to play with her, try to move and speak gently so you don't startle her. Give her plenty of time to react to things and remember that babies cannot concentrate for long. Never do anything she is not happy about.

Babies can only see clearly about 25cm (10in) from their nose.

Babies learn about things by putting them in their mouth, so always ask a grown-up if they are safe.

For the first few weeks, a baby probably has enough to do just getting used to her new surroundings. But she will soon start needing lots of things to look at and listen to.

When babies first learn to hold things, they like being given lots of different things to examine. However, they drop them very easily and don't know how to pick them up again.

Once the baby can sit up, she will be able to play with toys more easily.

Once he can crawl, you can give him things that roll.

# Babies in nature

Other babies are made, like people, by a mother and a father. In nature, when parents come together so that their sex cells can meet, it is called mating. The moment when the cells join together is called fertilization.

## Animals

Animals have their babies in a very similar way to people. During mating, sperm swim towards eggs inside the mother's body. If sperm fertilize the eggs, babies grow in the mother's womb. They are born through her vagina and feed on her milk.

Puppies stay in their mother's womb for nine weeks.

Most animals have more than one baby at a time.

## Birds

Baby birds grow outside their mother's body instead of inside. After mating, the mother bird lays her fertilized eggs. Babies grow in the eggs so long as the parents keep them warm by sitting on them.

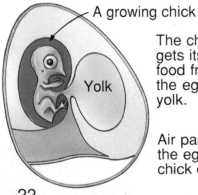

A growing chick

Yolk

The chick gets its food from the egg yolk.

Air passes through the egg shell so the chick can breathe.

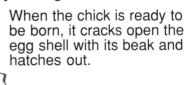

When the chick is ready to be born, it cracks open the egg shell with its beak and hatches out.

Eggs that we eat are unfertilized eggs. Chicks could not have grown in them.

## Insects

Insects lay eggs after mating and fertilization. Most baby insects do not look much like their parents at first. They go through a big change before they are fully grown.

A caterpillar hatches from a butterfly's egg.

The caterpillar changes into a pupa.

The pupa becomes a butterfly.

## Fish

Mother fish lay their eggs before they have been fertilized. The father then comes along and puts his sperm on them, and babies start to grow.

Baby fish in their eggs.

Two fish have hatched.

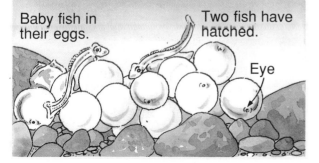

Eye

## Caring for the babies

Animals and birds look after their babies until they can manage on their own. Baby insects and fish have to fend for themselves from the start.

Many animals carry their babies out of danger by picking them up in their mouths or giving them a piggy back ride.

Parent birds feed their babies when they see their brightly-colored throats.

Babies snuggle up to their parents to keep warm.

Many animals keep their babies clean and show them affection by licking them.

# Index

animals 3, 22, 23
antibodies 18

birds 22, 23
birth 2, 3, 12-13, 17, 22
bottle-feeding 18-19, 20
boys 14, 17
breast-feeding 18
breasts 3, 11, 18
breathing 2, 5, 14

Caesarian 13
cells 4, 8, 16, 18, 22
chromosomes 16, 17
conception 10-11, 16, 17
contractions 12
crying 3, 20

diapers 19
doctor 6-7, 13, 14

egg cells 8, 9, 10-11,
   16, 17, 22
eggs 22, 23
eye color 15
eyesight 21

feeding 3, 14, 15, 18-19,
   22, 23

fertilization 10-11, 22, 23
fish 23

genes 16
girls 14, 17

hair 15
hatching 22, 23
heart 4, 5, 7, 13
hiccups 5
hormones 11, 12, 18
hospital 12, 13, 14, 15

incubators 15
insects 23

jealousy 20

kicking 5, 7

labor 12-13
love 10, 18

mating 22, 23
midwife 6-7
milk 3, 11, 18, 22
monitors 13

ovaries 8

ovum 8
oxygen 2, 5

penis 9, 10
periods 9, 11
placenta 5, 12
playing 21

sex 10
   cells 8, 9, 22
   chromosomes 17
sleeping 5, 19
soft patch 15
sperm cells 9, 10-11,
   16, 17, 22, 23
sterilizing 19

tampons 9
testicles 9
toys 21
tummy button 14
twins 17

ultrasound scanner 7
umbilical cord 5, 12, 14
uterus 2

vagina 8, 9, 10, 12, 22

First published in 1991. Usborne Publishing Ltd, Usborne House, 83-85 Saffron Hill, London EC1N 8RT, England. Copyright © 1991 Usborne Publishing Ltd.

The name Usborne and the device are Trade Marks of Usborne Publishing Ltd. All rights reserved. No part of this publication may be reproduced, stored in a retrieval system or transmitted in any form or by any means, electronic, mechanical, photocopying, recording or otherwise, without the prior permission of the publisher. Printed in Belgium. American edition 1991.

3

# DATE DUE

93-2423

j           Meredith, S.
QP251       Where do babies come
M4          from?
1991

                              09/94


DISCARDED

P9-CSU-789

# Medieval Legends

# Medieval Legends

*ADAPTED AND EDITED BY PHILIP S. JENNINGS*

*Introduction by Joseph E. Grennen*

*St. Martin's Press*

First Published in the United States by St. Martin's Press, Inc.
1983
10  9  8  7  6  5  4  3  2  1

Copyright ©1983 by J.K. & T., Inc. 212 East 18th St., New York, N.Y.
All rights reserved.

Designed by Nancy Ovedovitz.
Picture Research by Jamie Fitzgerald.
Printed and bound in the United States of America.
This edition for sale only in the United States of America, its
territories and dependencies.

**Library of Congress Cataloging in Publication Data**

Main entry under title:
Medieval Legends
1. Literature, Medieval          I. Jennings, Philip S.
PN667 .M42  1983          808.8'002          83-9713


ISBN  0-312-52726-8  N82I

# Contents

Illustrations 7

Introduction 9

Amleth's Revenge 13

The Death of Roland 21

Guigemar 27

Erec and Enide 41

La Belle Jean 53

The Story of Merlin 66

The Cursed Dancers of Colbek 77

Palamon and Arcite 81

Sir Gawain and the Green Knight 96

Parsival at the Castle of the Grail 112

The Death of Arthur 125

Eliduc 138

The Knight of the Swan                    147

The Dean and the Magician                 150

Andreuccio, the Young Merchant            154

Fra Puccio's Penance                      167

The Lustful Monk                          172

Melusina                                  177

Fra Cippola                               181

The Priest and the Blackberries           188

Suggested Reading                         190

Acknowledgements                          191

# Illustrations

*Page*

33 The White Hart. *Fourteenth Century Painting on Wood.*

34 The King Surprises the Lovers. *Fifteenth Century Illuminated Manuscript.*

51 Knights Proving Their Valor for Fair Ladies. *Fourteenth Century Manuscript.*

52 A Maiden with Many Suitors. *Fifteenth Century Arras Tapestry.*

69 Merlin and the Young Arthur. *Fourteenth Century Illuminated Manuscript.*

70 Lancelot Tells a Tale to Arthur as Guenever Looks on. *Fourteenth Century French Manuscript.*

87 Palamon and Arcite Spy Emily From Their Prison. *Fourteenth Century French Manuscript.*

88 A Royal Hunting Party. *Fifteenth Century Manuscript.*

105 Gawain and the Green Knight. *Fourteenth Century English Manuscript.*

106 Armorer Making a Hauberk. *Fifteenth Century Manuscript.*

123 The Vision of the Grail Appears Before the Round Table. *Fifteenth Century Manuscript.*

124 A Tournament Held for Arthur and His Court. *Fifteenth Century Manuscript.*

157 Andreuccio's Plight. *Fifteenth Century Manuscript of the Decameron.*
158 Revelers in a Tavern. *Fifteenth Century Manuscript.*
175 The Lustful Monk. *Fifteenth Century Manuscript of the Decameron.*
176 Hunting the Wild Boar. *Fifteenth Century Tapestry.*

# Introduction

he setting for the narratives included in this collection is the European world, including the British Isles, during the era that spanned the twelfth and fifteenth centuries. It was a time of tremendous intellectual ferment, of extraordinary accomplishments in art and architecture and of political and theological debates that culminated in wrenching reforms of civil and ecclesiastical institutions. It would be strange indeed if the turbulent events of the time found no echo in its literature.

These tales are in part exercises in poetic fancy — imaginative evocations of personal, social and political ideals that, in practice, generally remained beyond human reach; but they are also, in part, reflections of actual behavior. In our own day, for example, when it is the patriotic duty of a prisoner of war to attempt escape, we smile at the notion of medieval knights being bound by their word to remain in custody until their ransom has been paid; but the evidence of contemporary chroniclers, such as Froissart, strongly suggests that this ideal was borne out in practice. In such a light, it would be unthinkable for Sir Gawain, having given his pledge to Bercilac as a Christian knight, not to keep his rendezvous with what appears to be certain death.

Printing was not to be invented until almost the close of our period, and most of the literature of the sort here collected was presented orally to audiences who, whether aristocrats or commoners, would not have been proficient readers. It seems quite clear, for instance, that *Sir Gawain and the Green Knight* was intended for reading aloud by a minstrel, probably at some northern baronial court, and that, while it may have been read by individual preachers for inspiration, *The Cursed Dancers of Colbek* — a section of Robert of Brunne's long devotional work, *Handlyng Synne* — was ultimately designed for recital to a church congregation, most likely as part of a sermon on the vice of being a loose-tongued jangler. Sophisticated authors like Chaucer and Boccaccio, had, of course, a future audience of readers in mind, even though they occasionally read certain of their works aloud to groups of cultivated contemporaries.

The cultural ambience of these legends, from the loftiest aristocratic epic or romance, such as *The Death of Roland* or *Sir Gawain*, to the most blatantly cynical piece of anti-clerical satire, a tale like *Fra Cipolla*, was shaped by the omnipresence in medieval life of the two forces of religion and government — at the head of one the ruler or "prince," the apex of the feudal pyramid; and at the head of the other the Holy Father, the pope, presiding over complicated systems of ecclesiastical machinery designed to organize to the final degree the process by which Christian souls were to be kept on the straight and narrow path of virtue.

As subjects for literature both systems had their positive and negative aspects. The mythic conception of Arthur "the once and future king," was the inspiration for a large body of stories extolling by example the chivalric virtues of feudal allegiance, honor, generosity and courtliness. But the Arthurian myth also allowed for stories about lapses from those lofty ideals, such as the infidelity at the center of *Eliduc*. On the religious side, the example of Christ himself often lies close behind the deeds of knights like Gawain and Parsival, while the chasteness and obedience of the Virgin Mary is frequently reflected in the actions of virtuous women like the heroine of *La Belle Jean*. However, the baneful aspects of church administration — priests, pardoners, or friars, for example, who abused their offices for personal gain — generated an entire sub-class of tales centering on clerics who lie, fornicate, rage and steal. Boccaccio's *Fra Puccio* shows, as do most of Chaucer's tales in that vein, the genius for selecting and transmuting popular story into sophisticated art.

The themes in this collection vary widely. The mysterious workings of love coupled with that particularly medieval respect for the word, especially one's own word, produce tales that are "questions of love," such as *Eliduc*. Fascination with what seemed to be preternatural experience underlay a good many stories, particularly the so-called Breton *lais*, such as *Guigemar* with its enchanted boat and magical knots; while the constant presence of death, which stimulated an extensive theological literature on the "art of dying well," struck heroic literary chords in accounts of the deaths of heroic figures like Arthur and Roland. Finally, the conviction that the great Book of Nature had much to teach those who could plumb its mysteries, sent some authors to the world of animals, birds, even trees, for examples that might be turned into figurative emblems of human character traits. Hence the symbolic value of the successive hunts of deer, boar and fox in *Sir Gawain and the Green Knight*, as a means of defining the hero's three reactions to the lady's seductive advances.

Much of what has come down to us is, regrettably, anonymous. But much also can be confidently assigned to great medieval story-tellers known by name, some of whom, in fact, were socially prominent as well as extensively learned. Among the authors represented here are the German Wolfram von Eschenbach, the Frenchwoman Marie de France, the Italian Boccaccio, and the Englishmen Chaucer and Malory. It is only fair to say that the world view characteristic of this later medieval period has been studied in minute detail by historians, theologians, philosophers, and others, but it is also axiomatic by now that the most concrete, vivid sense of any age is that conveyed by its art, and particularly its literature. One who reads this collection will beyond all doubt be entertained in abundant measure, but he or she will also come to a fuller understanding of the yearnings, fears and dissatisfactions — the psychic life, in short — of the people of an age remote in fascinating ways from our own.

New York, 1983                                                            J.E.G.

# Amleth's Revenge

*This, the first recorded version of the Hamlet story, was written by Saxo Grammaticus, a Danish cleric, who set down this tale some 400 years before it inspired a young playwright named Shakespeare.*

eng has murdered his brother, the King of Denmark and the father of Amleth, and has married the queen. Amleth, the heir to the throne, feels that his life is threatened.

Seeing this, but not wanting to arouse his uncle's suspicions by intelligent action, Amleth behaved like a witless fool, pretending to have taken leave of his senses, by which ruse he not only concealed his intelligence but also saved his life. Day in and day out he sat listless at his mother's hearth, covered in dust and dirt, or flung himself on the floor and rolled in all the grime and filth. With befouled face and smeared visage he resembled a grotesque and ridiculous fool. His every word was utter nonsense, and all his actions denoted profound folly. In short, one would scarcely have thought him a man at all, but an absurd freak of some perverse fate. Sometimes he would sit by the hearth, poking the embers with his fingers, and twisting branches into crooks which he would harden in the fire and furnish with barbs to make them hold tighter. When asked what he was about, he would say that he was making spearheads for his father's revenge. This reply evoked no little amusement, all men deriding such an absurd and idle pursuit; but afterward this very work helped him to carry out his purpose. At the same time, it was his diligence and care that first aroused suspicion that all was a ruse on his part; for his very persistence in such a pastime revealed the hidden skill of the craftsman; and no one could believe that a simpleton would be so nimble-fingered and ingenious. Last, he would lay the hardened stakes in a pile and most carefully hide them.

For this reason, there were some who pronounced him sane enough, and said that he only concealed his intelligence under a show of simplicity, cunningly hiding his real mind beneath a feigned manner. The surest way of detecting his ruse (they said) would be to bring to him at some secluded place a fair woman who might tempt him to lust, for the natural desire for a woman's embrace was so intense that it could not be held back by cunning — the instinct too powerful to be subdued by guile. If then the apathy were feigned, he would forthwith seize the opportunity and yield to his strong desire. So men were commissioned who would ride deep into the forest with the young man, and there tempt him in this manner. Now among them it so happened that there was a foster brother of Amleth, who had not forgotten how they had been brought up together, and who rated the memory of their past fellowship higher than the present command. Thus, in joining the other appointed companions it was his intention to warn Amleth rather than to entrap him, for he had little doubt that certain death awaited him if he betrayed but the slightest sign of sanity, and especially if he embraced a woman in their sight: an outcome of which Amleth himself was well aware. When they bade him mount his horse he therefore deliberately seated himself the wrong way round, turning his back to the horse's head and his face toward its tail, and laying the reins round its tail, as if to check the horse's wild career from there. By this ingenious device he made a mockery of his uncle's trick and frustrated his evil design. Ludicrous it was indeed to see the horse run off unreined, with the rider holding on by its tail.

The company finally set off toward the place they had appointed for the meeting. On their way to that place they came down to the beach and his companions found there the rudder of a ship that had been wrecked, saying what a huge knife it was they had come upon. Amleth replied: "Ah, but that is for carving the biggest ham with," whereby he of course meant the wild ocean that the rudder matched. When they passed the sand dunes, and would have had him believe that the sand was flour, he answered that it had surely been ground by the beating of the surf. When his companions praised his reply, he retorted that he had indeed spoken shrewdly.

They now left him to himself, that he might more easily gain courage for the satisfaction of his lust, and the woman whom his uncle had intended for him came forward to meet him, as if accidentally, at a secluded spot. He would also have enjoyed her, had not his foster brother secretly revealed to him their schemes.

Having been forewarned by his former kinsman, he took the woman in his arms and carried her off to a remote and impassable fen. There he lay with her, and begged her earnestly to reveal it to no one. The young woman was as avid to promise silence as Amleth was to plead for it, for they had been friendly as of old, having been fostered together and brought up in the same charge.

They now accompanied him home again; and when all jestingly inquired if he had controlled his desire, he announced that he had enjoyed the maid.

They then questioned the maid, but she declared that he had done no such thing, and they accepted her denial, especially as the attendants were unaware of what had occurred.

Now all being confounded, and none capable of opening the secret lock of the young man's wisdom, a friend of Feng, one more gifted with assurance than with sagacity, spoke up and said that such unfathomable cunning could not be made to betray itself by ordinary stratagem—the man was too obstinate to be mastered by a common plot, nor would craftiness so versatile be caught in so simple a trap. Therefore, on deeper reflection he thought of a more subtle means, one which would not be difficult to apply, and which would surely discover all they desired to know. Feng was deliberately to absent himself on the pretext of an important errand, and Amleth was to be closeted alone with his mother; but first a man should be stationed in some concealed place, unknown to either of them, so that he might listen closely to what they talked of. For if the son had any wits at all, he would speak freely and openly in his mother's hearing, and would not fear to confide in her. He declared himself ready to do the spying himself, in case he be judged quick to advise but slow to perform. Pleased with this advice, Feng departed, pretending to go on a long journey.

Now the man who had given counsel went secretly to the closet where Amleth was admitted to his mother, and hid in the straw on the floor. Amleth, however, was equal to the plot. Suspecting the presence of an eavesdropper, he at first had recourse to his usual folly: crowing like a cock, beating his arms as if flapping wings, treading on the straw, and jumping on it to find out if anyone was hiding there beneath it. Feeling something firm under his feet, he thrust his sword into the spot, struck the eavesdropper who lay hidden there, and dragging him from his concealment slew him. Then he cut the body to pieces, boiled them in hot water, and flung them into the gutter for the pigs to eat, the miserable limbs being fouled in stinking mire.

Having thus frustrated this plot, he returned to the chamber; and when his mother set up a loud wailing and began to lament her son's madness, he cried: "How dare you, infamous woman, make such false complaints, which are no more than a cloak for your own grievous offense? Wanton like a harlot, you consented to a wicked and abominable marriage, incestuously embracing your husband's murderer, and kissing and caressing the man who slew the father of your child. So does the mare join with the stallion that triumphs; only brute beasts couple indiscriminately. And now, like them, you have wiped out the memory of your former mate. It is not without reason that I now behave like a fool, for I have little doubt that he who took his brother's life will proceed just as cruelly with his kindred. Better, therefore, to behave foolishly than to display one's wits, and so to save one's life by posing madness and frenzy. It remains my steadfast purpose to avenge my father; but I await a favorable opportunity and will bide my time. There is a time for all things; against a dark and pitiless heart one must use intelligence and ingenuity. For your part, you have no need to bewail my madness, but ought rather to grieve for your own shame. You certainly have cause to weep—not for others, but because you have suffered harm to your own soul. Now see that you hold your peace!" Thus scornfully did he chide his mother, recalling her to the path of virtue, and urging her to set past love above her present lust.

When Feng returned, he could nowhere find the crafty eavesdropper, though he searched long and diligently for him. No one had seen him anywhere. When Amleth, too, was asked jestingly if he had seen any trace of him, he replied that he had gone to the privy and, falling through the hole, had been smothered in filth, and so had been devoured by the pigs that went there. This statement contained only the bare truth, yet seemed to those who heard it so foolish that they ridiculed it.

Now Feng grew suspicious of his stepson, and being convinced of his guile resolved to make away with him, but dared not for fear of his uncle Rorik, as well as for fear of his wife; for which reason he found it expedient to request the king of Britain to slay Amleth, and by so doing feign innocence himself while another did the deed. Anxious to conceal his own cruelty, he thus chose to sully his friend's reputation rather than to bring disgrace on himself. Amleth, on departing from his mother, secretly charged her to hang the hall with woven tapestries, and in a year falsely to mourn his death, promising that he would return at that time. Two of Feng's retainers went with him, bearing a rod that was engraved with runes that enjoined the king of Britain to slay the youth who had been sent to him. But, while the others lay alseep, Amleth searched their belongings, found there the message, read the instructions, and, erasing the runes that were engraved on the rod, carved other symbols in their place, altering the words of the message so as to transfer the death sentence from himself to his companions. Besides averting his own doom and destruction, and plunging others into the misery intended for himself, he also falsely added, in the name of Feng, a petition to the king of Britain that he should give his daughter in marriage to the intelligent young man he was sending him.

Arriving in Britain, the envoys waited on the king and presented to him their letter, which they believed would encompass their companion's death but which contained their own death warrant. Betraying no sign of his intentions, the king hospitably invited them to a banquet. Here Amleth thrust aside everything which was on the king's table, as if the food offered to him were poor, to everyone's surprise abstaining from the rich feast, and touching neither food nor drink. All were amazed by this foreign young man who disdained the sumptuous dishes on the king's table and refused all the delicacies as if they had been poor peasant fare.

When the banquet was over and the king took leave of his companions for the night, he instructed one of them to steal into the bedchamber and secretly listen to the conversation of the foreign guests in the night. Now Amleth, when asked by his companions how it was that the evening before he had left all the feast untouched, as if it had been poison, replied that the bread had been saturated with blood, that the liquor tasted of iron, and that the meat reeked of corpses and had the rotten stench of the grave. Furthermore, he said that the king had the eyes of a slave, and the queen had exhibited three acts of a servant. Thus, it was not so much the banquet as the hosts that he had found fault with. His companions now held his old weakness against him, and taunted him with all manner of abuse for blaming what should be praised, speaking ill of what was good, affronting an excellent king and a gentle lady with shameless talk, and making a laughingstock of those who merited praise.

The king, when he heard this from his retainer, declared that whoever spoke thus must be either the wisest or most foolish of mortals, when in so few words he could display such perfect acumen. Summoning his steward, he asked where he had got the bread. The steward replying that his own baker had made it, the king asked where the corn had grown from which the flour had been made, and whether there was any sign that anyone had been slain there. He replied that near the king's palace was a field, strewn with the bones of slaughtered men, and bearing traces of former carnage; and that, expecting a specially good harvest from this, compared with the rest, he had sown it in the spring in hopes of a rich crop. Therefore, it might well be that the bread had caught a taint from the congealed blood. Hearing this, and believing that Amleth had spoken the truth, the king next inquired where the pork had come from. The steward replied that by neglect his pigs had escaped from their sty and had eaten the rotten corpse of a robber, and that this might be the reason why the meat had been tainted. Perceiving the truth of Amleth's words in this matter also, the king then asked what he had mixed in the mead. When he heard that it had been brewed from honey and water, he demanded to be shown the spring, and ordered men to dig there, and they found several rusty swords, which could have tainted the water.

Realizing now that Amleth had given good reasons for his fastidiousness, and supposing that in scorning him for the meanness of his eyes he had been alluding to his ignoble birth, the king went secretly to his mother and questioned her about his father. She replied that she had known no man save the king; but on threatening to draw the truth from her by torture, he learnt that he was the son of a slave. By this forced confession his doubts and the slighting of his birth by Amleth were confirmed. Ashamed at his own fate, but agreeably surprised by the young man's intelligence, he inquired of Amleth why he had imputed to the queen the habits of a slave. Annoyed though he indeed was because his guest, in the night's conversation, had found fault with his wife's courtly behavior, he was now forced to hear that she had been born a thrall. For Amleth said that he had observed three actions of a bondwoman in her. First, she had, like a servant, drawn her mantle over her head. Second, she had lifted up her gown when she walked. Third, she had picked her teeth with a splinter and chewed the scraps of food she dug out. Amleth also said that her mother had been a thrall taken in war, which fact enabled him to tell that she was as much a slave by birth as she was by habit.

The king esteemed Amleth's intelligence like the wisdom of heaven itself; he gave him his daughter in marriage and honored his word as evidence from above. In order to carry out Feng's bidding to the full, the king hanged Amleth's escorts the next day. This service Amleth interpreted as a wrong done to himself, and pretended to be angered by it, whereupon, the king, for blood money, gave him gold, which he melted down in fire and secretly poured into two hollow sticks.

Amleth dwelt with the king for a year, but then begged leave of absence and returned home, taking with him of the king's treasures only the two sticks filled with gold. Going ashore in Jutland, he laid aside his present conduct and resumed all his former habits, deliberately giving a ridiculous air to his manner in place of his normal behavior. Besmirched with filth, he entered the banquet hall, where his funeral celebration was just then taking place. All present were astonished, as his death had been falsely reported. Fear turned gradually to mirth as the guests ridiculed one another because the man whose funeral they were attending had suddenly appeared in the flesh amidst them. Then they inquired about his companions, and, showing them the two sticks he had brought with him, Amleth said: "They are both here." This observation was true, for although most of the funeral guests thought his words foolish, he showed them, in place of the hanged men, the blood money he had received for them. Later he joined the other cupbearers at table and plied the guests with liquor in order to increase the merriment; and so that his long dress should not hamper his movements, he fastened it round his loins with his sword belt. From time to time he deliberately drew his sword from its scabbard, wounding himself at the fingertips, whereupon the bystanders had a steel pin driven through the sword and scabbard. In order to carry out his plot in greater safety, he diligently filled the noblemen's cups, making them heavy and stupid with drink, lulling them into such a drowsy intoxication that they could not stand on their legs. They staggered about until they fell to rest in the king's hall, making their beds right in the banquet room. Finding them now in the state that suited his purpose, and so seeing his chance to obtain his revenge, he gathered up the crooks that he had previously made in his robe, and going with them into the banquet hall, where the nobles lay sprawling on the floor, vomiting in their drunkenness, cut the supports of the tapestries that his mother had made and that hung on the walls of the hall. Having cut down the hangings and laid them over the sleepers, he took out the crooked stakes, and fixed the hangings so thoroughly and tightly that none of those who lay beneath them had the strength to get up, struggle as he might. He then set fire to the house; and the fire spread far and wide, the flames leaping hither and thither and enveloping the whole house, so that the royal palace was reduced to ashes and all within perished, whether they lay fast asleep or made fruitless attempts to escape. Next he went to Feng's closet—he had some time before been conducted by his men to bed—and taking Feng's sword, which hung by his bedside, hung up his own in its place. Then, rousing his uncle, he told him that his nobles were perishing in the flames, and that Amleth was there with his old crooks, intending to exact due vengeance for his father's murder. At these words, Feng sprang from his bed, but failing to find his own sword, was cut down as he vainly endeavored to draw the other from its scabbard.

Valiant and of immortal memory was the hero who shrewdly behaved like a fool, and under a guise of madness with wondrous art concealed a superior intelligence; for by his stratagem he not only saved himself but also succeeded in avenging his father. Cunningly he defended himself and manfully he avenged his parent, so that it is hard to say which was the greater: his courage or his wits.

# The Death of Roland

*This excerpt, from the anonymous* Chanson de Roland, *portrays one of medieval literature's most famous heroes, the brave but arrogant Count Roland.*

he daylight ends, dusk turns to utter darkness, and our emperor, Charlemagne, sleeps. He is two hundred years old, and his tortured soul raises in his sleeping mind dire images. He sees himself in the pass at Sizer, sheer rock walls rising on either side, his ashen lance tight in his grip. Suddenly Count Ganelon, who made peace with the Saracens, seizes the emperor's lance and with fierce swings sends it in splinters toward heaven.

The emperor doesn't wake, but has another dream. He sees himself in his chapel, home in sweet France, and a wild boar is sinking its teeth into his right arm. Then he sees a leopard appear and maul him. But look! Suddenly a boarhound descends the chapel stairs and attacks the boar, ripping the beast's right ear from its head, and then sinks its teeth into the leopard. The barons of France call the struggle of the beasts supernatural. They wonder aloud to each other which beast will live.

The emperor doesn't wake.

Night passes and with the dawn, proudly, our Emperor Charlemagne rides among the troops.

"Lords of France, barons, look before us at those steep cliffs of stone, that narrow pass. Who will remain to stop our enemies from passing through here? What barons among us will make up the rear guard?" The emperor stares at the most powerful barons.

Count Ganelon speaks: "My stepson Roland. You have no braver subject; none fiercer."

Our emperor snaps his head toward Ganelon, cold stares fill a silence, and says, "You are the devil himself, hellish vapors rule your mind. If you think Roland should be the rear guard, whom do you think should lead us?"

Ganelon says, "Oger, the Dane, who else could better lead us? None that I know."

Count Roland speaks, "Stepfather, I must now feel warmly toward you, for you have brought it about that I shall guard the rear of our holy emperor's army. Our emperor will not lose one single palfrey horse, not one war horse, no mules, no gold that hasn't been purchased with swords and lances."

"I know what you're saying is the truth," Ganelon says.

Roland looks at the narrow pass and turns to his stepfather. His words are full of anger: "You vile miscreant, you nothing. Did you think I would allow the glove of my oath to protect this pass fall to the ground, like you let the staff of your oath to make peace with the enemies drop into the fire? My hands don't shake with fear, stepfather, and I make no peace with my enemies."

"Just emperor," Roland says, turning to Charlemagne who is two hundred years old, "give me the bow you're holding, and I promise no one will in truth be able to say I dropped it, as my stepfather dropped the staff when he promised to make peace with our enemies."

Our emperor hears this and bows his head, pulls fiercely at his beard, rips hairs from his mustache, tears fill his eyes. He weeps. He turns to his nephew Roland.

"Brave Roland, dear nephew, you know very well I'll leave half of the army with you. You will be safe."

Roland says: "No. May God cut me down if I discredit my ancestors with such cowardice. I will keep with me only twenty thousand men, good men. Take your army through the pass now. You needn't worry, you have no reason to fear any man, any army, while I live."

Count Roland mounts his battle horse. His companion Oliver rides over next to him, and now comes Gerin to join them, and now the fearless Count Gerer. Gerard of Roussillon and Duke Gaifer on their war horses ride over and join the company. The Archbishop says: "By my head, Roland, I am with you in the rear guard."

Roland and his company choose twenty thousand men.

The hills are high, the valleys dark, the passes covered with shadows. That day with mourning the emperor and his army move slowly through the treacherous pass. The sound of their movement can be heard for fifteen miles. They arrive finally in sweet France and are riding into Gascony, Charlemagne's kingdom, and they are remembering their lands and their wives, their servants and their children. They are weeping for joy, each man in the troops, for they have been away a long time making war. But the Emperor Charlemagne is weeping more than any other, for he has left his nephew in the treacherous passes of Spain. Pity is wrenching at his heart, tears flow without stop. He cannot help weeping like a child.

Duke Naimes is riding beside our emperor. He says: "My lord, our holy emperor, why is your grief so great?"

Charlemagne says: "I feel wronged that you ask me that. I can't keep myself from weeping. Ganelon is destroying sweet France. An angel sent a vision into my dreams last night, and I watched as Ganelon took my lance from between my fists and shattered it into pieces. It is because of Ganelon that my nephew guards our rear, with only twenty thousand men. If I lose Roland I will never be able to replace him."

Our emperor is weeping uncontrollably, and a hundred thousand Franks are being seized with pity, and with fear for Count Roland and his party of brave men. Vile Ganelon has betrayed Roland, for while making peace he took great gifts from the pagan king: gold, silver, silk, camels, lions, precious gems. When Ganelon went to make peace with the pagan King Marsiliun, he betrayed his stepson. Marsiliun raised his sword to kill Ganelon, and Ganelon said:

"Don't kill me. If you want the Emperor Charlemagne to stop making war against you, you must kill his nephew Roland. Charlemagne will never fear anything as long as Roland lives. I will fix it so that Roland stays behind the French army in the rear guard. Kill him and Charlemagne will no longer make war with you."

The pagans are arming themselves in Saracen hauberks, thick as chains, and strapping on their swords, helmets and shields. Vermilion pennants are hanging from their lances, and they are riding in close formation. The day is clear, the sun bright as heaven, and a hundred thousand flashes of light are glinting off the pagans' armor. A thousand pagans are sounding their trumpets, and the men in the rear guard now hear the din.

Roland's companion Oliver says: "My friend, it sounds like the pagans plan to engage us in battle."

Roland answers his companion Oliver: "I hope to God they are, and it is our duty to fight them, to suffer hardship for the sake of our emperor. Let us tell our twenty thousand men to fight with everything they have, for when they sing of this battle in the future the song should be a good one. Christians are right and pagans are wrong. Let us set them an example even heathens without souls will admire."

Oliver is climbing to the top of a peak. He is at its summit now, and his eyes take in the pagan host. He shouts to Roland: "A huge host is approaching. I see a hundred thousand flashes of light coming from as many shields and hauberks, and a cloud of dust the size of a fiefdom. This will be a bitter battle for the French. Vile Ganelon has betrayed us."

Count Roland answers his companion Oliver: "Ganelon is my stepfather — I won't allow you to speak ill of him."

Oliver has come down from the peak and is telling the French host what he has seen: a hundred thousand pagans ready to do battle. Countless legions are approaching; the French are greatly outnumbered. Oliver says: "Roland, my friend, sound a blast on your ivory horn. Charlemagne will hear it and return with the troops."

Roland says: "Never. Sounding my ivory horn would be an act of cowardice that would ruin my fame in sweet France. We will stay here and fight, even to our deaths. Black will be the soul of any man who flees."

The battle is fierce and bloody. Each Christian is fighting against ten pagans. The grass and dust and rocks are covered with blood, severed limbs, dead pagans and Christians, dead horses.

Roland sees the French being slaughtered, and says to his companion

Oliver: "This is a fierce fight; I'm going to sound my ivory horn, for Charlemagne will hear it."

Oliver says: "Blowing your ivory horn now would be an act of cowardice. When I asked you to blow your ivory horn you arrogantly refused, and if you hadn't Charlemagne would have heard it and we wouldn't now be trampling our dead comrades in this battle. The dead around us could have been saved. All of us here are doomed, my friend, and this is the last day of our friendship as surely as the last of our lives."

The Archbishop says: "Roland, Oliver — don't fall to foolish arguing. Sound your ivory horn even though we are dead within the hour. The French will hear it and return here. They won't be here soon enough to save our lives, but they can avenge us on the Saracens and save our bodies from the wolves and those black birds circling overhead."

Count Roland is blowing his ivory horn, and it sounds long and loud. It echoes off the hills and passes through the valleys. Thirty leagues away, Charlemagne hears it.

The emperor says: "That is the sound of Roland's ivory horn. He wouldn't sound it unless the French were in battle fierce, unless, if I know my nephew, he sees his death this hour."

Count Roland is blowing his ivory horn, and blood is gushing from his mouth. The veins in his forehead have burst, and the mighty sound stops the French in their tracks. All the French are silent.

Charlemagne says: "Seize Ganelon, and hold him here like a vile criminal. Have our lowliest cooks surround him with long knives. He has betrayed the men of sweet France. Roland is dying at the hands of the Saracens; Ganelon will die by the hands of his friends."

The sun is low, the hills high, great clouds of dust hang over the field of battle. All of the French are dead except Count Roland. His brains are flowing out his ears. He staggers among the corpses, looking for Oliver, the Archbishop, the noble dead. He feels death overcoming him. To the east he sees a cloud of dust: the Saracens fleeing. To the west he sees another cloud: Charlemagne returning with the French Army. Among the corpses he sees a small, grassy mound. A pine tree stands at the top of the mound, and beneath the tree are four great stones of marble. Roland crawls to the mound, carrying his sword Durendal. He strikes a stone with all his failing might, for he wants to break his sword. No Saracen will ever have it, or claim he took it from Roland while he still lived.

Count Roland strikes the stone, but his sword neither shatters nor scratches, but bounces up toward the sky. Roland sees that his sword will not be broken. He speaks to it:

"Ah Durendal, beautiful, blessed Durendal. Your hilt is full of holy relics: a piece of the Virgin's dress, one of St. Peter's teeth, traces of St. Basil's blood, three strands of St. Dennis' hair. Is that why you won't break? While I still live no pagan will ever possess you, for it is right that you be in the hands of Christians. With you I have conquered lands for the emperor."

Count Roland feels his life flowing out of him, and he lays down on the green grass, his head pointing toward the land of the enemy. Memories flood his dying brain, memories of lands he conquered, of sweet France, of Charlemagne. He cannot stop his tears, and begins to confess:

"Heavenly Father, save my soul even though I have sinned greatly. You saved St. Lazarus from death and Daniel from the lions. Have mercy on a dying knight, forgive his sins both great and small."

Count Roland is holding his right glove up toward heaven. Saint Gabriel is taking it from his hand. Angels and Cherubim are hovering over the knight, and Charlemagne from five leagues away sees a brightness in the dust.

Count Roland is dead, and from the field of battle his soul is rising through the firmament.

# Guigemar

*Magical happenings and devices aid and confound Guigemar, who represents, in Marie de France's allegorical story, the process of growing from adolescence into maturity.*

t that time, Hoel ruled Lesser Brittany, which was as often at war as at peace. The lord of the Leonnais countryside was a vassal named Oridial, whom the king saw with great favor, for he was a courageous knight. Oridial and his wife had two children, a daughter and a son. The damsel was named Noguent. The young lord, Guigemar, was the most beautiful child in the kingdom. He was adored by his mother. His father also was devoted to him.

When the youth was old enough, Oridial sent him to serve his king. Guigemar was a brave and wise valet. All who knew him grew to love him. When the time came, the king dubbed him a knight and rewarded him richly with armor and a horse, exactly what Guigemar prized most. Then Guigemar left the king's court, showering his friends there with gifts as he departed. He set off to make his name in Flanders, where there were always conflicts and combats to be fought.

Nowhere in Burgundy, Lorraine or Gascony, not even in Anjou, could a man his equal be found. He had only one flaw: nature had left him without a desire to love. There was no lady or virgin, no matter how beautiful, no matter how noble, who would not willingly have received him should he have sought her. Many even made advances to him, but he felt not the slightest desire for any of them. Friends and strangers alike gave him up for lost.

When he had earned much glory the young baron returned to his homeland to see his father, his king, his sister and his good mother, who had all long awaited his coming. He had been with them about a month when one day he felt the desire to go hunting, a sport he greatly enjoyed.

In the middle of the night, he had his men awakened: his knights, his hunters and his beaters. At dawn they entered the forest on the scent of a great stag. They released the dogs. The hunters ran ahead, Guigemar came riding after. A squire carried his bow, his knife, his quiver. As he rode, Guigemar sought a target for his arrows. Deep in the brush he spied a doe and her fawn. Startled by the barking dogs, the doe sprang into the clearing. She was entirely white, with a stag's horns growing from her brow. He stretched his bow and shot, striking her in the breast. She fell to the ground, but, uncannily, the arrow rebounded and wounded Guigemar, hitting him with such force that it went through his thigh right into his horse's side. He was forced to dismount. He fell into the harsh grass beside the wounded doe. She was so badly injured that she would soon die.

Shuddering and grieving, she spoke to him: "Alas, I am dying! But you, vassal, who have wounded me, let this be your destiny: the wound in your thigh shall never heal! Neither herb nor root nor witchcraft nor potion shall cure you until you are healed by a woman. She will suffer, for love of you, more pain and grief than any woman has ever suffered. And you, in turn, will suffer so much for her that all lovers, past, present and future, shall marvel at it. Go away now from this place! Leave me in peace!"

Guigemar's wound was very deep. What he had heard alarmed him, for he had never met a woman whose love he desired. There was nothing left for him to do but die. But dying did not appeal to him at all. He called to his squire: "Quickly, my friend, spur your horse! Tell my comrades to come back." The squire went off in great haste, leaving Guigemar behind.

He bitterly contemplated his lot. Trembling and groaning from the pain, he bound his thigh tightly with his shirt. Then, remounting, he left, hastening to be far away, for he did not want his men to catch up to him. They might interfere or try to detain him. Down a green pathway he disappeared into the forest, which, at length, opened out into a meadow.

Crossing the open country, he came to the edge of a cliff, high above tidal waters. He found an arm of the sea which formed a natural harbor. In it was a single vessel; Guigemar could see its unfurled sail, and found it very beautiful. But the knight was astonished. He had never heard that a ship could land in that region. He approached and went down to the shore. With great difficulty he climbed aboard. He thought he would find men there guarding the ship, but there was no one at all.

The ship was in very fine condition, so perfectly tarred both inside and out that the seams were invisible. The pegs and handholds were made of ebony, the sail of silk. Amidships was set a bed whose legs and frame, in the style of Solomon, were inlaid with gold and cypress and the finest ivory. The coverlet was sable, lined in Alexandrian purple, its quilt of silk, woven with gold. The other bedclothes were priceless beyond description. Of the pillow, only this can be said: it was so soft that whoever lay his head there would never be grey. Two candelabra of the finest gold (even the smaller of the two was worth a fortune) were placed at the prow of the ship. Each held a lighted taper.

Guigemar marveled at all this. He was suffering from his wound. He lay down on the bed to rest. But when he rose to leave, he could no longer return to land, for the ship had already reached the high seas, carrying him swiftly away from it. A strong, gentle wind swelled the sail.

There was no hope of returning. He was very distressed. He knew not what to do. His wound was very painful. It is not surprising that he was dismayed: he would have to go where the ship took him. He prayed to God to watch over him, to use His powers to bring him safely to shore and to protect him from death. Then he lay down again on the bed and fell asleep.

That day he had suffered the worst of his pain. At nightfall he would reach the place of his healing, at the foot of an ancient fortress, the capital of its realm.

The lord who governed there was a very old man, and he had a beautiful wife, of high estate — honest, courteous and docile. He was inordinately jealous, for it is nature's law that all old men are jealous, afraid of being cuckolded.

The surveillance he kept her under was strict. At the foot of the castle there was an orchard that went down to the water's edge — completely enclosed by a wall of green marble, very high and very thick. This wall had but one gate, which was guarded night and day. On the far end the sea stretched to the horizon; no one could enter or leave from that side without a boat.

It was there that the lord, to keep his wife safe, had built her chambers, and under all heaven there were none more beautiful. All around her bedroom walls were painted murals of Venus, the goddess of love, shown teaching a woman how to honor her husband and loyally to serve him. In her hand she held Ovid's *Art of Love*, opened to the passage that claims each being is a slave to the laws of love. Venus was throwing the book into the fire, and cursing forever all those who henceforth would read it or follow its teachings.

It was here the lord kept his lady locked up. He had given her a virgin to serve her who was his own niece, the daughter of his sister. The two women had grown very close. The maid amused her mistress when the lord was away, and until he returned, neither man nor woman entered the orchard. Nor could his lady leave. A hoary old priest kept the keys to the gate, said mass for the lady and brought her dinner. Had he not lost his nether member, the lord would have been jealous of him too.

On the day Guigemar arrived, the lady went into the orchard. She had slept after dinner and now wanted to be amused. The virgin went with her. They were talking together, looking out at the sea, when they saw the boat, coming in with the rising tide, headed straight to the shore. But they could see no one at the helm.

The lady sought to flee. Her face grew flushed with fear. It is no wonder she was frightened. But the damsel, who was braver, reassured her and comforted her, then ran right down to the spot where the ship was landing. Casting off her cloak, she climbed aboard, where she found no living being, except for the sleeping knight. She stopped and stared at him and seeing how pale he was, believed him to be dead.

Returning to her lady in haste, she reported her adventure and the sad discovery of the dead man. The lady answered, "I want to see him. If he is dead, the old priest will help us bury him. If he is alive, he will tell us his story." They returned together to the ship without further delay. The lady walked first, followed by the maiden.

Going aboard, the lady went straight to the bed and stopped. Seeing the knight, she began to cry over the body lying there, his beautiful face, his youthful misfortune. Putting her hand on his chest, she felt that it was warm, and that a strong heart was beating under his ribs.

The knight awoke, stared at her, and then greeted her with joy, for he realized that he had reached land. The weeping lady returned his greeting kindly, asking him whence he came, and if he had been exiled because of war.

"My Lady," he answered, "it is not that at all. Would you like me to tell you my adventure? I will hide nothing from you. I come from Lesser Brittany, where this very day I was hunting in a wood. I shot an arrow at a white doe, but the arrow rebounded and wounded me so badly in the thigh that I think I shall never heal. The doe began to grieve, cursed me and cast a spell on me. She swore that I shall never be cured except by a woman whom I must love. But I know not where to seek her. When I heard the doe's malediction, I fled from the woods. I saw this ship in a harbor; I climbed aboard. It was madness, for the tide immediately carried it out to sea, and now I know neither where I am nor where I should go, nor am I able to steer the ship, for I am wounded. Fair Lady, I beseech you, in the name of the Lord, have pity on me and counsel me."

She answered thus: "Be not afraid, fine lord. This fortress belongs to my lord and master, as does the countryside around. He is a rich man, of ancient lineage, but he is very old, and I feel honorbound to warn you that he is eaten up with jealousy. He keeps me a recluse behind these walls. Here I live, night and day; here I have my chambers, my chapel, and the friend you see here beside me. There is only one entrance, and an old priest keeps the key, may he burn in Hell! I cannot leave this place without his permission or without orders from my lord. In spite of that, if you would like to stay here until you can walk again, we can easily hide you, and willingly serve you."

Guigemar thanked the lady kindly, saying he would remain with them. Rising up from his bed, he stood alone; he hardly even needed their help.

The lady took him into her chamber, where she made the young man lie down on the bed of the handmaiden. She brought water in a golden basin, and washed the wound on his thigh, cleaning away his spilled blood with a piece of soft linen. Then she bandaged his wound tightly. When food was brought to them that evening, she put aside enough for him to eat. Thus, he could satisfy his hunger, and slake his thirst. But now love had pierced his heart. Henceforth he was besieged. So mad with love was he for the lady that he even forgot his homeland. His wound no longer pained him, yet he sighed in new anguish. He begged the lady to let him sleep. She left him and went away, burning with the same fire that ate away at Guigemar's heart.

Left alone, the knight was pensive and miserable. He had not yet realized what was happening to him, but of one thing he was sure: if the lady did not cure this new wound, he would surely die of it.

"Alas," he sighed, "what shall I do? I'll go find her, I'll beg her to take pity on a poor invalid, abandoned by all. If she rejects my plea, and pridefully scorns me, my fate will be either to die of pain or to languish all the days of my life." Then he wept. But soon, little by little, he came to a new resolution: he decided to suffer in silence, as we must all do when we have no choice. All night long he lay awake sighing, worrying, running through his mind her words, her ways, her changing eyes, her beautiful lips, which had captured his heart. Through clenched teeth he begged for mercy. It took all his strength not to call to her. If he had known that love also tortured her, it would have eased the anguish which left him pale.

For though he was ill with love of her, the lady was not immune. In the grey dawn before daybreak, she rose, lamenting that she had not slept at all. All night long she'd been tormented by love. The maiden sleeping at her side guessed easily from her face that she loved the knight they were hiding in her chamber, but she did not yet know if he loved her.

The lady went into her chapel to pray, and the maiden came to the knight. She sat down by his bed. He spoke to her: "My friend, where has my lady gone? Why has she gotten up so early?" And he fell silent, sighing.

Then the maiden understood everything, and hesitated no more. "My Lord, you are in love. You need not hide it any longer, for you may be well received. She is lovely; you are charming — it would be a perfect match if you were never to leave each other. But he who wishes to love my lady must promise her everlasting honor."

This was his answer: "I am so enamored that this sickness will surely

pour aler a chambre et quant il teuint pour
vne fenestre que estoit endroit le lit sa fille et
quant illot ouuerte si mist sa teste dedans.

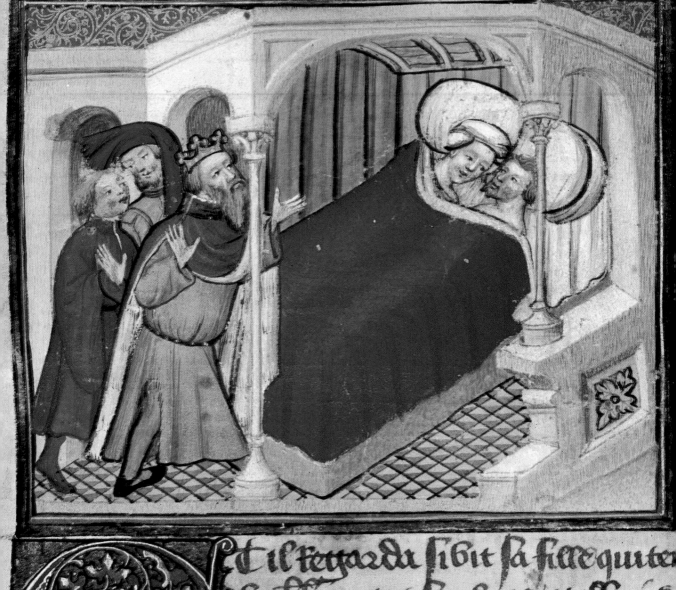

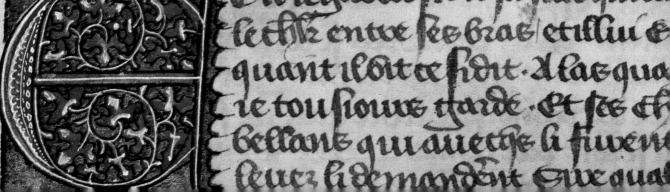

Et il regarda si bit sa fille qui ter[...]
le chief entre ses bras / et illui et
quant il sit ce sist. Alas qua[...]
ie tousioure garde. Et ses ch[...]
bellant qui auecthe li suiuen[...]
seur li demandent. Sire qua[...]

consume me if no one comes to my aid. Oh, kind friend, advise me. What must I do?"

The damsel comforted the knight with great gentleness and assured him she would do all she could. How goodhearted and noble she was!

And so, having heard mass, the lady returned, her heart pounding, and hastened to see what Guigemar was doing, whether he was awake or asleep. Saying nothing, the maiden took the lady to the knight's bedside, so that each in their own time could reveal their thoughts. He greeted her; she him. Both were very troubled.

He dared not speak because he was from a faraway land. He was afraid if he declared his love she would hate him and drive him away. But he who hides his sickness cannot be cured, and love is like a wound that does not show. It is, moreover, a natural malady, and all the more tenacious for being so. Some men make light of it, like faithless couriers, who seduce far and wide, telling the world of their conquests. But that is not love but folly, evil and lechery. On the contrary, he who finds true love must serve it, cherish it and follow its commands.

Guigemar loved desperately. If he did not quickly find relief, he would be doomed to live in misery. Love made him brave. He revealed his thoughts.

"My Lady," he said. "I am dying for you. My heart is in great anguish. If you will not cure me, I shall surely die. O lovely Lady, do not send me away!"

When she had heard him out, she answered as was fitting, laughing as she spoke:

"Friend, it is not my habit to grant my favors so quickly!"

"My Lady," he responded, "may God be thanked! But I pray you listen to what I am going to say: only an easy woman feigns hesitation — to enhance her worth and make her suitor think she is new to the game. But when a woman of good character, worthy and intelligent, finds a man who suits her she must not show false pride with him. She loves him and takes her pleasure with him, and before anyone suspects anything they will have passed many happy hours together. Wonderful Lady, let this arguing be finished!"

The lady saw that he spoke the truth, and on the spot granted him her love and kissed him. Guigemar was the happiest of men. They lay down together and talked, often kissing and embracing, and enjoyed all the other caresses lovers know so well.

For a year and a half, Guigemar lived by her side. Their life was one long delight. But fortune cannot be conjured. Its wheel can turn in only a few hours. He who was above goes under, another rises. And so it happened to them, for they were caught.

One summer morning the lady was lying beside her lover, kissing his mouth and his face, saying, "Dearly beloved, my heart warns me that I will lose you. We will be seen and found out. If you die, I too, will die, but if you escape, you'll find another love, and I'll be left alone with my sorrow."

"My Lady," Guigemar answered, "you must not say that! May I never find joy or peace again if I seek consolation with another! You have nothing to fear."

"Then make a pledge to me, my friend: give me your shirt. I will tie a knot in the tail, and you may love only the woman who can untie the cloth."

He handed her his shirt. She made a knot that could not be untied without tearing or cutting the cloth, and then she gave it back to him. In taking it, he made the same request: that she pledge herself to him by letting him buckle a sash around her flanks, next to her naked skin. The man who could open the buckle without breaking it or tearing the cloth, would have the right to love her. Then they kissed and thought no more about it.

And that very day they were glimpsed by a chamberlain. May the Devil burn him! His lord had sent him to seek the lady. When he could not get into her room, he spied by the window and saw them playing. Returning to his lord, he told him all, and the lord, hearing as much, was angrier than he had ever been. Calling three friends, he went straight to the chamber, broke down the door and found the knight inside. In his fury he ordered Guigemar killed.

Guigemar stood up, unafraid. Taking a long pole used for hanging out laundry, he waited for them. Blows were going to fall: they would all be injured before they could touch him.

The lord observed all this. Then he asked him who he was, who his father was, and how he entered there. Guigemar told of his journey, the injured doe, his wound, the ship.

The lord announced that he did not believe a word of it. If it were true, then Guigemar could make his ship come back, and if it did, the lord would let him sail away free. If he survived, the lord would be sorry to hear it. Better he should drown.

He gave his word to Guigemar and together they went down to the shore, where they saw the boat waiting for him. They made him climb aboard. The boat drew out to sea and sailed away. Sighing, crying, lamenting the loss of his lady, Guigemar raised prayers to the Almighty, asking that his death be quick, and that he never reach a port on whose shores his lady wasn't waiting. He cared more for his lady than for his own life. Guigemar languished in sorrow until the ship that bore him arrived in a port near his native land. He left the phantom boat immediately.

Almost as soon as he disembarked, Guigemar encountered a boy whom he had helped raise, a handsome young man he used to tutor years ago. The young boy was following a mounted knight, riding behind him on a war horse. When the boy recognized Guigemar, he instantly dismounted and offered his tutor of old the horse. Guigemar rode along with the boy and the knight, and the more of Guigemar's friends they met the more rejoicing there was. Even though he was given much honor in his own land, he was sorrowful. His friends urged him to marry, but he wouldn't even look at a woman, not for love nor for money, unless she could untie the knot in his shirt.

Word of the knot in Guigemar's shirt spread throughout Brittany, and both maids and maidens arrived and tried to undo it. They all failed.

Now I want to digress and tell of the lady Guigemar loved to the exclusion of all others. After consulting with his advisors, her jealous husband locked her in a marble tower, where her days were made dreary, and her nights even worse. Pain, anguish, lonesomeness, suffering — there are not words capable of describing the lady's stay in that dark tower. She was imprisoned there for two years, I've heard, and in all that time she didn't have so much as a moment of happiness. She talked to her lover as though he, her sole desire, could hear her: "Oh Guigemar, my lord, I would that I never laid eyes on you, for I'd rather die quickly than languish in this torture. If I could break free of this prison, my love, I would go to where your magic boat sailed off and drown myself in the sea."

One day she discovered — and no one could describe her surprise and elation when she did — the door to her prison unlocked. She managed to get outside. No one was about. She went to the harbor and, again surprised, found Guigemar's magic boat. The boat was anchored in the exact spot where she planned to throw herself into the sea. She went aboard, thinking, "this is where my lover vanished." Suddenly she fell down in a swoon, and when she awoke she found the boat had arrived at a port, in Brittany, in the shadow of a fortified castle.

The castle's lord, Meriaduc, was waging war with a neighboring lord, and had been awake since dawn, planning attacks on his enemy. Through a window he spotted the magic ship, summoned a chamberlain and rushed down to explore the mysterious vessel, where they found the beautiful, fairylike woman. He brought the girl to his castle, wondering as he did who had put her on the mysterious ship, and almost immediately felt he loved the girl as much as he had ever loved a woman.

Meriaduc had a younger sister, a beautiful maiden in her own right, whom he ordered to care for the fairylike lady. Meriaduc's sister dressed the girl in noble clothes, waited on her hand and foot, attended to her every wish; but despite all the attention she was given the girl remained as sorrowful as she was when still in prison. Meriaduc relentlessly pleaded with the girl, offering to make her his queen, promising her everything. She refused all of his offers, and when he asked why she showed him her belt, explaining that she could love no man but he who could undo it. When Meriaduc heard this he turned red with anger. He told the girl that someone else in Brittany avoids taking a lover until one proves able to undo a knot in his shirt. "I'll bet you tied that knot yourself," the lord angrily said.

The lady almost fainted when she heard this and would have fallen if Meriaduc hadn't caught her in his arms. With a knife he cut the laces of her tunic and tried to untie the knot in her belt. He couldn't. Meriaduc summoned every one of his knights, ordering them as they arrived to undo the lady's knot if they could. They couldn't.

This process went on until it was time for a tournament, at which Meriaduc challenged his enemy. He gathered among his ranks as many knights as he could. He was certain Guigemar would appear for the tournament, especially as he had invited him urgently, asking the bold knight not to let him down during his hour of need. With a hundred knights following him, Guigemar arrived, and Meriaduc entertained him royally. Meriaduc sent two knights to fetch his sister, and to command her to bring with her to the banquet the fairylike lady, whom he loved. Beautifully dressed, the two women entered the banquet hall. When the lady heard Guigemar's name she almost fell to the floor in a faint, but Meriaduc's sister held her up. Guigemar stood up when he saw the lady.

"Could it be," Guigemar exclaimed, "that someone has brought to me my only love, my beautiful lady, my life, my heart? It can't be she. I know well that women often resemble each other, and I'll not upset myself with false hopes, although I'll gladly speak to her." Guigemar kissed the lady and asked her to sit beside him. Meriaduc watched the two of them like a hawk, grumbling to himself at the sight of them.

"My lord Guigemar," Meriaduc said cheerfully, "why don't you give this beautiful lady a chance to untie the knot in your shirt."

"Certainly," Guigemar answered, gesturing as he did so to one of his chamberlains, who was in charge of the shirt. Guigemar gave the knotted shirt to Meriaduc's sister, who tried for all she was worth but couldn't undo the knot. The lady, of course, recognized the knot, and hoped in her heart she would be given the opportunity to try to untie it. Saddened, Meriaduc realized the fairylike lady was longing to have a chance at the knot. "Fair lady," Meriaduc finally said, "try your luck at untying Guigemar's knot."

The lady untied the knot instantly, and Guigemar was so stunned he could scarcely speak, although he managed, at last, to say, "Is it you? Please speak to me truthfully. Let me look at your bare body, and the belt I knotted around you." He put his hand on the lady's hips and, right through her clothes, felt the belt. "Dear love," he cried, "we are the luckiest of mortals. How did you come here?"

The lady told Guigemar of her painful two years in prison, her lucky escape, how she found his ship and how it brought her here, where Meriaduc treated her royally but asked continually for her love. "My love," Guigemar shouted, "embrace me, give me your heart forever, marry me and you will be the bride of the happiest, luckiest man on earth. Cure me forever of living without love."

Then Guigemar turned toward those assembled at the banquet and said

"My lords, I have found the love I thought I had forever lost. If Meriaduc will allow me to take her as my wife I will pledge myself to him as a vassal for two years, three years if need be, and I will pledge as well a hundred knights."

"My handsome friend," Meriaduc replied, "the war I'm waging with my neighbor isn't so full of strife that I would give up this lady for a hundred and one knights. This beautiful lady was magically delivered to the door of my castle, and I intend to care for her. I will defend her until my death, even if I have to defend her against you."

Even before Meriaduc finished speaking, Guigemar ordered all of his knights to mount. Embittered, Guigemar and his knights rode away. Guigemar's knights, one by one, declared their loyalty to him; and in unison all hundred knights vowed that failing to help Guigemar now would be the greatest of dishonors. They promised to follow wherever he led them. By nightfall the party of knights reached the castle of Meriaduc's enemy, who rejoiced that Guigemar and his knights had come over to his side of the battle.

Next morning the troops rose even before dawn, donned their armor and rode out of the castle. Guigemar led the knights in an assault of Meriaduc's stronghold, but the castle was so fortified they weren't able to take it. Even though it wouldn't fall, Guigemar led his knights and besieged the castle further, refusing to leave until it had fallen. Eventually, however, the knights defending the castle consumed all the food inside of it; and when they tried to foray out and obtain food Guigemar stormed the fortress and captured it. He killed Meriaduc, then, amid cheers, led his lady away, bringing all his pain to its end.

I have told you the story of Guigemar, which many tell as they strum a lyrical harp. The music is beautiful to hear.

# Erec and Enide

*This excerpt, from Chretien De Troyes' long narrative of the same name, epitomized the conflict between marital love and knightly prowess.*

rec loved Enide with such a tender love that he cared no more for arms, nor did he go to tournaments, nor have any desire to joust. He spent his time in cherishing his wife, and made of her his mistress and his sweetheart. He devoted all his heart and mind to fondling and kissing her, and sought no delight in other pastimes. His friends grieved over this, and often regretted among themselves that he was so deep in love. Often it was past noon before he left her side; for there he was happy, say what they might. He rarely left her society, and yet he was as generous as ever to his knights with arms, dress and money. There was not a tournament anywhere to which he did not send them well-apparelled and -equipped, whatever the cost might be. All the knights said it was a great pity and misfortune that such a valiant man as he was wont to be should no longer wish to bear arms. He was blamed so much on all sides by the knights and squires that murmurs reached Enide's ears how her lord had turned craven about arms and deeds of chivalry, and that his manner of life was greatly changed. She grieved sorely over this, but she did not dare to show her grief, for her lord would at once take affront if she should speak to him of the matter. So it remained a secret, until one morning as they lay in bed, where they had had sport together.

There they lay in close embrace, like the true lovers they were. He was asleep but she was awake, thinking of what many a man in the country was saying of her lord. And when she began to think it all over, she could not keep back the tears. She began to survey her lord from head to foot, his well-shaped body and his clear countenance, and she said: "Alas, woe is me that I ever left my country! The earth ought by right to swallow me up when the best knight has completely abjured all his deeds of chivalry because of me. And thus, in truth, it is I who have brought shame upon his head. Unhappy man!"

Erec was not sound asleep and heard what she had said. Surprised to see her weeping, he said, "Tell me, my precious beauty, what has caused you woe and sorrow? It is my wish to know. Take care to keep nothing back, tell me why you said that woe was me, for you said it of me and no one else. I heard your words plainly enough."

"Sire," said she, "I know nothing of what you say."

"Lady, why do you conceal it? You have been crying; and you do not cry for nothing. And in my sleep I heard what you said."

"Ah fair sire, you never heard it; it was a dream."

"Now you are coming to me with lies. But if you do not tell me the truth now, you will come to repent of it later."

"Sire, since you torment me thus, I will tell you the whole truth. In this land they say it is a great pity that you have renounced your arms; your reputation has suffered from it. They all go about making fun of you, calling you recreant. Do you suppose it does not give me pain to hear this scorn? It grieves me even more that they put the blame for it on me. They all assert that I have ensnared you. You must choose another course and silence this reproach."

"Lady," said he, "you are in the right, and those who blame me do so with reason. And now prepare to take the road. Rise up from here, dress in your richest robe, and order your palfrey saddled."

Sad and pensive, Enide obeyed. Erec summoned a squire and bade him bring his arms to arm his body withal. When they had put on his hauberk, a valet laced about his head a helmet fluted with a band of gold, shining brighter than a mirror. Then he took his sword and strapped it on, ordering a squire to bring his bay steed.

So they departed. Erec leads his wife he knows not whither, as chance dictates. "Ride fast," says he, "and don't speak to me of anything you may see, unless I address you first."

"Sire, it shall be done." But to herself she laments: "My lord has turned against me; and I am not so bold as to dare to look at him."

A knight who lived by robbery issued from the wood. With him were two companions. All three were armed. Enide saw them and was seized with great fear. She calls to Erec: "Sire, there come riding after us three knights. I fear they will do you harm."

"What's that you say? You have been very bold to disdain my command and prohibition. This time you shall be pardoned, but you will not be forgiven again." Then, turning his shield and lance, he rushes at the first knight. Both give spur and clash together, holding their lances at full extent. But the robber missed Erec, while Erec used him hard, for he knew well the right attack. He strikes him on the shield so fiercely that he cracks it from top to bottom. Nor is his hauberk any protection; Erec pierces it and crushes it in the middle of his breast, and thrusts a foot and a half of his lance into his body. When he drew back, he pulled out the shaft. The robber fell to earth. He must needs die, for the blade had drunk of his life's blood. Then one of the other two rushes forward towards Erec, threatening him. Erec firmly grasps his shield and attacks him with a stout heart. They strike upon the emblazoned shield. The knight's lance flies into bits, while Erec drives his through the other's breast. He will give him no more trouble. Erec spurs at an angle toward the third robber. When the latter saw him coming he began to make his escape. But his flight is of small avail; Erec hits him squarely on his painted shield and throws him to the ground. Giving the three no further heed, he then took their horses and tied them together by the bridles. He bade Enide lead on and drive the horses in front of her.

Erec and Enide entered the wood and journeyed without halting. While traversing the wood, they heard in the distance the cry of a damsel in great distress. When Erec heard the cry, he said to Enide: "Lady, there is some maiden who goes through the wood calling aloud. I am going to hasten and see what her trouble is. Await me here, while I go yonder."

Leaving her alone, he made his way until he found the damsel. The maiden was rending her garments, and tearing her hair and her tender crimson face. Erec begs her to tell him why she weeps so sore. The maiden cries and says: "Sire, I wish I were dead. My lover has been led away prisoner by two wicked giants who are his mortal enemies. He is in great peril of death. Noble knight, I beg you to save my lover, if now you can lend him any aid. You will not have to run far, for they must still be close by."

"Damsel, I will follow them. If the giants let him live until I can find him, I intend to measure my strength with theirs."

"I shall always be your servant if you restore to me my lover."

Then Erec started at a gallop and followed a path covered with the giants' footprints. He caught sight of them before they emerged from the woods; he saw the knight with bare limbs, mounted naked on a nag, his hands and feet bound as if he were arrested for highway robbery. The giants had no lances, shields or whetted swords, but they both had clubs and scourges, with which they were beating him so cruelly that already they had cut the skin on his back to the bone. Down his sides and flanks the blood ran, so that the nag was all covered with blood down to the belly. Between two woods in an open field Erec came up to them. "My lords," said he, "for what crime do you treat this man so ill and lead him along like a common thief? It is a monstrous insult to strip a knight naked, and bind him. Hand him over to me, I beg of you."

"Vassal," they say, "what business is this of yours? You must be mad to make any demand of us. If you do not like it, try and improve matters."

Erec replies: "Indeed, I like it not, and you shall not lead him away so easily. I say whoever can get possession of him, let him keep him. I challenge you: take your positions."

"Vassal, you are mad. Even if you were four instead of one, you would have no more strength against us than one lamb against two wolves."

Erec replies, "Many a man boasts loudly who is of little worth. On guard now, for I am going to attack you."

The giants were strong and fierce, and held in their clenched hands big clubs tipped with iron. Erec went at them, lance in rest. He strikes the foremost of them through the eye so deep into the brain that blood and brains spurt out at the back of his neck. That one lay dead. When the other saw this, he had reason to be furious. He went to avenge him — with both hands he raised his club on high so as to strike the knight squarely upon his unprotected head. But Erec watched the blow and received it on his shield. Even so, the blow quite stunned him and almost made him fall to the earth from his steed. The giant thinks to strike him again quickly; Erec, however, had drawn his sword, and struck the giant so hard upon the neck that he split him down to the saddle-bow. His bowels scattered upon the earth, and his body fell full length, split into two halves.

Then Erec unbound the knight, he said, "Noble knight, thou art my liege lord, for thou hast saved my life. Sire, I wish to do thee homage; henceforth, I shall always accompany thee and serve thee as my lord."

"Friend," Erec says, "for your service I have no desire; I came here at the insistence of your lady, whom I found in this wood. I wish to present you to her now. As soon as I have reunited you with her, I shall continue my way alone. But first, I would fain know your name."

"Sire, as you wish. My name is Cadoc of Tabriol. Since I must part from you, I should like to know who you are and of what land."

"Friend," Erec replies, "that I will never confide to you. Never speak of it again."

They continued their way until they came to the knight's maiden. Her joy knew no bounds when she saw her lover again. Taking him by the hand, Erec presented him to her with the words: "Grieve no longer, demoiselle! Behold your lover."

And she with prudence replied: "Sire, by right you have won us both. But who could ever repay half the debt we owe you?"

Erec answered: "My gentle lady, no recompense do I ask of you. To God I now commend you both; for too long, methinks, have I tarried here." He turns his horse and rides away as fast as he can. He comes back to the road where Enide is awaiting him, and they ride on.

They rode till nightfall without coming to any town or shelter. When night came they took refuge beneath a tree in an open field. Erec bids his lady sleep, and he will watch. She replies that she will not. It is for him to sleep who is more weary. Well pleased at this, Erec accedes. Beneath his head he placed his shield, and the lady took her cloak and stretched it over him from head to foot. Thus he slept and she kept watch, never dozing the whole night, but holding the horses tightly by the bridle until the morning. Erec rises early and again they take the road, she in front and he behind.

At noon a squire met them in a little valley, accompanied by two fellows who were carrying cakes and wine and some rich autumn cheeses to those who were mowing the hay in the meadows belonging to Count Galoain. The squire was a clever fellow, and when he saw Erec and Enide, he perceived that they must have spent the night in the forest and had had nothing to eat or drink, for within a radius of a day's journey there was no town or city, no castle or place of refuge. So he formed an honest purpose and turned his steps toward them, saluting them politely and saying: "Sire, I presume you have had a hard experience last night. I offer you some of this white cake, if it please you to partake of it. The cakes are of good wheat; I have wine and cheese too, a white cloth and fine jugs. If you feel like lunch, you need seek no further."

Erec got down from his horse and said: "Gentle friend, I thank you kindly; I will eat something." The young man knew well what to do: he helped the lady from her horse; the boys with the squire held the steeds. Then they go and sit in the shade on the greensward. The squire relieves Erec of his helmet, unlaces the mouthpiece; then he spreads out the cloth on the thick turf. He passes them the food. They help themselves and gladly drink of the wine. The squire serves them and omits no attention.

After the repast, Erec was courteous and generous. "Friend," says he, "I wish to present you with one of my horses. Take the one you like the best. And I pray it may be no hardship for you to return to the town and make ready there a goodly lodging." The squire chooses a horse and springs up by the left stirrup to gladly do the knight's will. He rode to the town at top speed; he engaged suitable quarters. Then he returned to them. "Now mount, sire," he says. Your lodgings are ready." Erec and Enide followed him into town where they were received with joy.

When the squire had done for them all the honor that he could, he rode off in front of the Count's bower to the stable. The Count and three of his vassals were leaning out of the bower, when the Count, seeing his squire mounted on a steed, asked him whose it was. And he replied that it was his. The Count, greatly astonished, says: "How is that? Where didst thou get him?"

"A knight whom I esteem highly gave him to me, sire," said he. "He is by far the handsomest man I ever saw."

"I presume that he is not more handsome than I," replied the Count.

"Upon my word, I dare maintain that he is fairer than you. And there comes with him a lady so fair that never a lady was half so fair as she." When the Count hears this news, he desires to see if this is true or false.

The squire ran ahead to tell Erec that the Count was coming to visit him. Erec's lodging was rich indeed — the kind to which he was accustomed. There were many tapers and candles lighted all about. The Count came attended by only three companions. Erec, who was of gracious manners, rose to meet him and exclaimed: "Welcome, sire!" And the Count returned his salutation. They sit down side by side upon a soft white couch, where they chat with each other. The Count makes him an offer and urges him to consent to accept from him a guarantee for the payment of his expenses in the town. But Erec does not deign to accept, saying he is well supplied with money, and has no need to accept aught from him. They speak long of many things, but the Count constantly glances about in the other direction, where he caught sight of the lady. Because of her incomparable beauty, he fixed all his thought on her. He looked at her as much as he could; he coveted her, and she pleased him so that her beauty filled him with love. Very craftily he asked Erec for permission to speak with her. "Sire, I ask a favor of you, and may it not displease you. As an act of courtesy and as a pleasure, I would fain sit by yonder lady's side. With good intent I came to see you both, and you should see no harm in that. I wish to present to the lady my service in all respects. Know well that for love of you I would do whatever may please her."

Erec was not in the least jealous and suspected no evil or treachery. "Sire, I have no objection. You may sit down and talk with her." The lady was seated about two spear-lengths away from him. And the Count took his seat close beside her on a low stool. Prudent and courteous, the lady turned toward him. "Alas," quoth he, "how grieved I am to see you in such humble state! I am sorry and feel great distress. But if you would believe my word, you could have great wealth and advantage. Such beauty as yours is entitled to great honor and distinction. I would make you my mistress, if it should please you and be your will; you would be my mistress dear, and lady over all my land. When I deign to woo you thus, you ought not to disdain my suit. I know and perceive that your lord does not love and esteem you. If you will remain with me, you would be mated to a worthy lord."

"Sire," says Enide, "your proposal is vain. It cannot be. I will never be false to my lord, or conceive any felony or treachery towards him. You have made a great mistake in making such a proposal to me. I shall not agree to it in any wise." The Count's ire began to rise. "You disdain to love me, lady? Upon my word, you are too proud. Neither for flattery nor for prayer will you do my will? It is surely true that a woman's pride mounts the more one prays and flatters her, but whoever insults and dishonors her will often find her more tractable. I give you my word that if you do not do my will there will soon be some swordplay here. Rightly or wrongly, I will have your lord slain before your eyes."

"Ah, sire, there is a better way than that you say. You would commit a wicked deed if you killed him thus. Calm yourself again, I pray; for I will do your pleasure. You may regard me as all your own, for I am yours and wish to be. I did not speak as I did from pride, but to learn and prove if I could find in you the true love of a sincere heart. But I would not at any price have you commit an act of treason. My lord is not on his guard; and if you should kill him thus, you would do a very ugly deed, and I should have the blame for it. Go and rest until the morrow, when my lord shall be about to rise. Then you can better do him harm without reproach. Have me carried away by force; then my lord will rush to my defence. Seize him or strike his head off, if you will. I have led this life long enough; to tell the truth, I would rather feel your body lying beside me. Of my love, you may rest assured."

The Count replies: "It is well, my lady! God bless the hour that you were born; in great estate you shall be held."

Well Enide knows how to deceive a fool, when she puts her mind to it. The Count now rises from her side and commends her to God a hundred times. He also takes his leave of Erec.

Erec slept until daylight. Enide realized that she might hesitate too long, so she rises and draws near to her lord to wake him up. "Sire," says she, "I crave your pardon. Rise quickly, for you are betrayed. The Count hates you because he desires me. Last evening he would have killed you had I not assured him that I would be his wife. You will see him return here soon to do the foul deed." Thus Erec learns how loyal his wife is to him. The horses are saddled and they set out upon their way.

Meanwhile, there entered the house a hundred knights well-armed, and very much dismayed they were to find Erec no longer there. The Count learned that the lady had deceived him. He discovered the footsteps of the horses, and they followed the trail, the Count threatening that nothing could keep him from having Erec's head when they find him. Then they plunge on at topmost speed, filled with hostility toward him who had never laid eyes on them and had never harmed them by word or deed. At the edge of a forest they catch sight of him before he is hidden by the trees. All rushed on in rivalry. Enide hears the clang of their arms and sees that the valley is full of them.

"Ah, sire," she cries, "the Count and his hosts are attacking you!" Erec straightway turns about, and sees the Seneschal drawing near upon a horse both strong and fleet. They ride to meet each other and strike upon each other's shield great blows with their sharp and trenchant swords. Erec causes the steel sword to pierce his body through and through, so that his shield and hauberk protected the Seneschal no more than a shred of dark-blue silk. Next, the Count comes spurring on, a strong and doughty knight. He showed his exceeding boldness by rushing on ahead of all his men more than the space of four crossbow shots. The Count and Erec come together with the clash of arms. First the Count strikes him with such violence upon the breast that he would have lost his stirrups if he had not been well set. He makes the wood of his shield to split so that the iron of his lance protrudes on the other side. But Erec's hauberk was very solid and protected him from death without the tear of a single mesh. The Count breaks his lance, but Erec strikes him with such force on his yellow-painted shield that he ran more than a yard of his lance through his abdomen, knocking him senseless from his steed. Then he turned and rode away without further tarrying.

Straight into the forest he spurs at full speed. The Count's host paused a while over those who lay in the middle of the field. The Count opens his eyes a tiny bit; he realizes now what an evil deed he has begun to execute. "My lords," he says, "I bid you all advance no further. Return now, quickly! I have done a villainous deed, and I repent of my design. I well deserve this woe. Never was there a better knight born of mother than he. I command you to go back." Back they ride, disconsolate, carrying the lifeless Seneschal on his shield.

Erec rides at great speed to the place where Enide was awaiting him in great concern. Erec comes up to her and Enide, seizing the stirrup, springs joyfully up on to the horse's neck. Erec embraces and kisses and gives her cheer. In his arms he clasps her against his heart and says: "Sweet sister mine, my proof of you has been complete! Be no more concerned in any wise, for I love you now more than ever I did before; and I am certain that you love me with a perfect love. From this time on, forevermore, I offer myself to do your will just as I used to do. And if you have spoken ill of me, I pardon you and acquit you of both the offense and the word you spoke." Then he kisses her again and clasps her tight. Now Enide is not ill at ease when her lord tells her that he loves her still. Evening has come; rapidly through the night they ride, and they are very glad that the moon shines bright.

# La Belle Jean

*The personification of a faithful wife, Jean represents, in her allegiance and her shrewdness, the power of female practicality in a male-oriented world of chivalric ideals.*

here was a knight who dwelled in the marches of Flanders and of Hainault. This knight was wise in counsel, brave of heart, very steady and trustworthy. His wife was a fair lady of whom he had one daughter, young and fresh, a maid twelve years old named Jean. Many sweet words were spoken about this maiden, because in all the land there was none so fair. Her mother prayed often to her lord that he should give the girl in marriage; but his thoughts were so busy on the running of tournaments that he didn't consider the betrothing of his child, even though his wife always admonished him on his return from the jousts.

This knight had a squire, a young man named Robert, the bravest squire in any Christian realm. His prowess and his merit were such that often he aided his lord to bear away the prize from the tournaments in which he rode. So great was his value that his lady spoke to him thus:

"Robert, my lord cares more for these joustings than for any words I speak, which grieves me, since he should take care to wed this daughter of mine. I pray you, therefore, for love of me, that you tell him what ill he does and how greatly he is to be blamed for not marrying off his own fair child; there is no knight in these parts, however rich his estate, who would not gladly welcome such a bride."

"Lady," said Robert, "you have spoken well. Very readily will I speak therefore, and since my lord often asks me for my counsel, I have every hope that he will heed my words."

"Robert, you will find me no miser if you do this task."

"Lady," said Robert, "your prayer is reward enough for me. Be assured I will do all I can."

"I am content," answered the lady.

Now shortly after this the knight prepared to journey to a tournament very far from his land. When he came to the field, he (with a certain knight in whose company he rode) was joined to one party; his banner was carried to his lord's lodging. The tilting began, and the knight did such deeds, by the cunning service of his squire, that he bore off the honor and the prize of the tourney from one end to the other. On the second day the knight made ready to return to his own country. Robert took him to task and blamed him greatly for not bestowing his fair daughter in marriage. At the end of hearing this many times his lord replied:

"Robert, you and my lady give me no peace in the matter of the marriage of my daughter; but I see and know of no one in my land to whom I am content to give her."

"Ah, sir," cried Robert, "there is no knight in your realm who would not receive her with joy."

"Robert, fair friend, they are worth nothing, not one of them; neither will I bestow her there with my goodwill. I know of no man in the world who is worthy of her, save one man only, and he, alas, is no knight."

"Sir, tell me his name," answered Robert, "and I will find means to speak to him so urgently that the marriage shall be made."

"Verily, Robert," returned the knight, "it seems to me you are greatly desirous that my daughter should be wed. Since you are so ready to party at her wedding, she shall soon enough be married if you agree to it."

"Sir, right willingly will I consent to it."

"Do you pledge your word to that?"

"Truly, sir, I do."

"Robert, you have served me faithfully, and I have always found you skilled and true. Such as I am, you have made me; for by your aid at the tournaments I have gained five hundred pounds of rent. This I owe to you, and I pay my debt by giving you my fair daughter, if you are willing to take her hand."

"Ah, sir, for the love of God, don't say this. I am too low a man to reach at so high a maiden."

"I will bestow her on you, and for her dowry she shall bring four hundred pounds from rent of my lands."

"Oh sir, you mock me."

"Robert, be assured this is no jest."

"Neither my lady nor her kin will consent to it."

"This matter concerns none of them. I give you my glove and I invest you with my dowry; this glove is my warrant for its delivery."

"Sir," said Robert, "I will not refuse so good a gift, since it is given with so true a heart."

The knight and his squire returned to the knight's house. When he entered his wife received him and said:

"Husband, for the love of God, what about the marriage of our maid?"

"Dame, you have spoken so often of this matter that I have betrothed her already."

"Sir, to whom?"

"Verily, I have pledged her to a man who will be loyal and true. I have given her to Robert, my squire."

"To Robert! Alas the day! He is but a naked man. There is no knight in all the land, however noble, who would not have taken her gladly. Robert shall not have her!"

"Dame," answered the knight, "have her he shall. With good will or bad; I have made a covenant with him and I will carry out my bargain."

When the lady heard these words she sought her chamber and wept. After her tears were shed she sent for her brothers and kinsmen and told them about her lord's decision.

"Lady," they said, "what have we to do herein? We will not go counter to your lord, for he is a stout knight, weighty of counsel and heavy of hand. Besides, he can do what he likes with his daughter. We will not hang a shield about his neck for this cause."

"Alas, never may my heart find happiness again if I so lose my child. At least, fair lords, tell him that he acts wrongly and not after his own honor."

"Lady," they said, "this we will do full willingly."

So they sought out the knight and acquitted themselves of their task; and he answered them cleverly.

"Fair lords, I will defer this marriage on such understanding as I now declare. You are great lords, rich in gold and lands. Also, you are near of kin to my fair daughter. If on your part you will endow her with four hundred pounds of rent on your lands, I will disavow this bond of marriage and will wed the girl according to your wise counsel."

"In the name of God," they answered, "would you spoil us of all the wealth in our purses?"

"Since you won't do this thing, please suffer me to do as I will with my own."

"Sir, we will, with right good mind."

Then the knight sent for his chaplain, and before him affianced Robert and his daughter together, appointing a certain day for the marriage. Robert prayed his lord that he would dub him knight, since it was not seemly that he should take a wife so fair and of such high station till he was of her degree. His lord agreed with a glad heart, and granted him his desire; after that he married the maid with great joy and festival.

At the hour Sir Robert was made knight he spoke thus to his lord:

"Sir, once when I was in peril of death, I vowed to seek Saint James's shrine on the morning after the day I gained my spurs. I pray, be not angry with me if tomorrow, after the wedding, it becomes my honor to go there directly, for in no way will I fail to observe my vow."

"Sir Robert, if you do this to spite my daughter, and go lonely upon your road, very rightly will you be held to blame."

"Sir, it is God's will, I shall soon return, but I must go on peril of my soul."

When a certain knight heard these words, he reproached Sir Robert for parting from his bride at such an hour.

"Truly," said the knight, who was named Raoul, "truly if you go to Saint James's shrine, leaving so fair a bride a wedded virgin, very surely will I win her love ere you return. Certain proofs will I give that I have had my way with her; and to this I pledge my lands against the lands our lord has granted you, for mine are fully worth the rents of yours."

"My wife does not come of a race to deal me so low a wrong, and since I give no credence to your words, I will take your wager."

So the morning after the bridal mass, incontinent and without tasting the wedding meats, Robert parted from the hall and set forth on his way, a pilgrim to Compostella.

Raoul, meanwhile, was hot in thought as to how he might gain the wager and have the fair lady. He sought to meet with an old dame who attended on her, promising her that if she brought him in such a place and hour that he might speak privily to Madame Jean, and have his will, then never in her life would she be poor.

"Sir," said the crone, "you are so lovely a knight, so sweet in speech and courteous, that verily it is my lady's duty to set her love upon you. It will be a pleasure to toil in your service."

So the knight took forty sous from his pouch and gave them to her. He then bade farewell, but the crone tarried in that place, and when her lady entered from the church, where she spent much time upon her knees praying to God to bring her lord home again, she said to her:

"Lady, tell me truly, when my lord went to Compostella did he leave you a maid?"

"Why do you ask such a question, Dame Hersent?"

"Because, lady, I believe you to be a virgin wife!"

"That I am, nor do I know a woman who would be aught else in my case."

"Ah, lady, the pity of it! If you but knew the joy that women have in the company of the man they love, you would say there is no fonder happiness to be found on earth. But you are alone. However, I know a knight, comely of person, who asks naught better than to set you on his love. He is very rich and far lovelier than the shameful villain who has left you in this plight."

While the crone was speaking, the lady, who was but a woman, felt her senses stir within. She inquired who this knight could be.

"Who is he? God above! One has no fear to cry his name! Who should it be but Sir Raoul, the sweetest heart in all the world."

"Dame Hersent," said the lady, "you will do well to let these words be, for I have no wish to do myself such wrong, neither come I of such stock as goes after shame."

Thus ended their discourse.

Presently Sir Raoul came again to the crone and she told him of her lady's answer.

"So should a virtuous lady reply," said the knight, "I pray, speak again with her, for the archer does not wing the bird with the first arrow. Take these twenty sous and buy yourself a petticoat."

Then said the crone that in no wise could she snare the bird, but that for the great love she bore him, this thing would she do—that she would arrange for him to be alone with her lady in the house, and then he could act according to his pleasure. Raoul agreed eagerly.

"Sir," said the old woman, "come again in eight days; on this day my lady will bathe in her bower. You may then come privily to her chamber and have your desire of her, whether she cry yea or nay."

Hard upon this arrived letters from Sir Robert that he would be at the castle on Sunday, his vow to Saint James duly consummated. On the preceding Thursday, therefore, the crone caused the bath to be heated in the bower. The lady disarrayed herself to enter. Then the crone sent to Raoul to make haste, and he promptly responded; he entered the bower and saluted the fair Jean.

"Sir Raoul," she said, "of a truth I thank you for this courtesy, yet you might have asked if such a visit would be to my wishes. Accursed you are, a most ungentle knight!"

"Madame, for God's sake, have pity on me. I am dying of love for you. Lady, as you hope for grace, so grant your grace to me."

"Sir, never will I grant you my love. Know well that if you do not leave me alone, my father will requite the honor you rob from me. I am not such woman as you think."

"Nay, lady, is it so indeed?"

"Yes, and surely."

Sir Raoul sprang forward and, clasping her in his arms (he was very mighty), bore her toward the bed. As they strove he saw beneath her right breast a black spot; here was certain proof that he had had to do with her, he thought. Just then his spurs caught the valence about the foot of the bed and they fell together, the lord below and the lady above; whereupon she seized a billet of wood from the nearby hearth and smote him on the head. Blood dropped on the rushes from the wound, a wound so deep and large that Raoul no longer wished to play. He arose from the floor and departed to his own lodgings and sought a surgeon for his hurt. The faithful lady resumed her bath, complaining to Dame Hersent about the villainous knight.

Very great was the feast that the father of the fair lady held for Sir Robert's homecoming on Sunday. Many a lord was bidden to his hall, and among these Sir Raoul. He bandaged his face as best he could and went to the hall, where all day long the party sat at meat and drink. Afterward, they rose to dance. But after the dinner, Sir Raoul demanded of Sir Robert that he should pay his wager, since he had had to do with his wife, by sign and token of a certain black spot beneath her right breast.

"Of that I know nothing," answered Sir Robert. "For I have not looked so boldly upon her."

"By faith, take heed and do me justice herein."

"That I will."

When the night came and when the lady received him as becometh every wife to receive her husband, Sir Robert observed her curiously and marked the spot on her white body. His grief was immense. In the morning he sought out first Raoul, to own that he had lost the bet, and then he went to his wife's father to tell him of his loss and his disgrace. That very same evening Sir Robert saddled his palfrey and sallied forth on the road to Paris, intending to sojourn there for some three days.

Very stricken was the fair lady that her lord had thus fled. She wept and lamented her widowhood until her father entered her chamber. He said it were better she had never wed; she had brought shame to him and to all her house, and he told her how and why. When she heard this thing she was sick at heart; she swore she had never done such a deed; but her words profited nothing, for though a woman give her body to be burned, none will believe her clean of sin once such blame is laid on her.

Early the next night the lady rose from her bed, took what wealth she had in her coffer, and mounted a palfrey. Her dainty tresses were sheared to the shoulder and she was clad as a boy. In this manner she came to Paris, a squire searching for her lord and husband. There she met Sir Robert. Her heart was full as she drew close to salute him.

"Fair friend, God give you your desire," Sir Robert said.

"Sir," said she, "from whence come you?"

"I am of Hainault."

"Sir, and whither you go?"

"Forsooth, I know little where my path may lead me, nor do I have a home. Fortune hails me unkindly; I have lost the thing I most loved in the world. But tell me, what is your name and where are you bound?"

"Sir, my name is John. And you, sir, what is yours?"

"John, my name is Robert."

"Sir Robert, join me to your company as squire, and I will serve you."

"I would do so gladly, John, but I have little money in my pouch; ere three days are gone I must sell my very steed. I may take no squire."

"Sir, be not troubled," John assured him. "On my part I have with me nearly ten pounds, and these are as your own."

"Fair friend, thanks, and thanks again."

The two comrades rode at a brisk pace to Montlhery, where John found meat for his lord and they ate together. When they had eaten they sought their chamber, the knight lying on a comfortable bed, and John sleeping in another at his feet. The next day they journeyed to Marseilles upon the sea, but to their grief they heard no rumors of any adventures or wars. There was no arming in all the land.

"John," Robert said, "what shall we do? You have lent me much money. I will repay it even if I have to sell my palfrey to discharge the debt."

"Sir, there remain yet to us one hundred sous. Grant me leave to turn our good horses into better money. With this I will make French bread, and I little doubt that we shall gain our money and livelihood besides."

"John, do as you think best."

John sold the two horses for ten pounds. With these he bought corn and carried it to the mill. Afterward he bought baskets and set to work at his oven to bake good French bread. So white and so fresh were these loaves that he sold more than the best baker of the town. He prospered so greatly that within a few years he had put by one hundred pounds for their needs.

"Would it not be good to rent a large house, with cellarage for wine, that we might offer hostelry and lodging to wealthy folk from abroad?" John now suggested.

"John," Sir Robert answered, "your will is mine; every reason have I to be content with you."

The inn and bakery flourished and they made plenty of money. John clad his lord in costly raiment, and Sir Robert sat at meat and drink with the most honorable of the town. His companions also marveled at the abundance of his stores. In four years John had put by more than three hundred pounds, besides the furnishings of the inn and bakery, which were well worth another fifty pounds.

Sir Robert and John dwelt as citizens in Marseilles for six years. The business prospered exceedingly. John was beloved of all his neighbors; men spoke almost too well of him, and he maintained his lord in such estate it was marvelous to see. When the end of the seventh year drew nigh, John sought occasion to speak soberly to Sir Robert.

"Sir, we have been so fortunate in our dealings that we have gained nearly six hundred pounds in money and in silver vessels. You are my true lord and never, please God, will I take another. Let us therefore return to your country; perhaps we may find adventure and profit there too."

"By my faith," Sir Robert answered, "I thank you heartily, John. I hold you not as servant, but as comrade and friend. All this is not mine but yours; you have earned it. What you require of me, that is my pleasure. However, as to returning to my own country, I know not what to say. So much have I lost there, it can never be made up to me."

"Sir, fret not over your loss. I shall gather enough for me and for you. Please God, you shall hear good news when you come into your own land."

"John, I will do that which pleases you and lodge wheresoe'er you will."

So John sold the house and bought horses for the journey. They bade farewell to their neighbors and to the most worshipful citizens of the town, who grieved sorely at their going. In less than three weeks they drew near their own country. Sir Robert caused it to be told to his lord, whose daughter he had wedded, that he was approaching.

The lord was merry, for he hoped his daughter might be with her husband. He greeted Robert warmly, but when he could learn no tidings of her, his mirth turned to sorrow. For the nonce, he made a rich banquet and bade his knights to the feast. Among them was Sir Raoul, who still held Sir Robert's lands. During the festivities Robert told John the story of the wager and the manner in which Raoul had spoiled him of his property.

"Sir," said John, "challenge him to combat as a false traitor; I will fight the battle in your stead."

"John, this you shall not do!"

Thus they left the matter till the morrow, when John said to Robert that he intended to speak to the father of his wife. So they sought the lord, and John said to him:

"Sir, you are, after God, the lord of my master, Sir Robert. As you know, a wager was made between him and Sir Raoul. Sir Raoul spoke falsely and is a most disloyal and treacherous knight, for never had he part or share in your daughter's love. All of which I am ready to prove upon his body."

"John, fair friend," Robert interrupted, "this business is mine alone, nor because of it shall you hang shield about your neck."

So Sir Robert threw down his glove and Sir Raoul tendered gage of battle in return, though but fearfully; for needs must he defend himself or be proclaimed recreant and traitor. The date for the ordeal was set for fifteen days thence without appeal.

Then John, who was more sweetly named Madame Jean, went to a cousin in the house of her father, a fair maid of some twenty years. To her Jean revealed the whole matter, telling her the entire story from beginning to end. She also asked her to keep it hidden until such time as she should make herself known to her father. The cousin promised to conceal her, and put her own chamber at Jean's disposal. There for the two weeks before the battle Madame Jean bathed and perfumed herself and took her ease, for well had she reason to look her fairest. She caused women to shape closely to her figure four goodly gowns; one was of scarlet, one of green, one of peacock blue, and one of trailing silk. Thus with rest and peace she came once more to the fullness of her beauty, and was so dainty, fresh, and lovely that no lady was her peer in all the world.

During these days Sir Robert sorely missed his squire, for he knew nothing of his fate. Nevertheless, on the appointed day he got into his harness and prepared for the battle.

The two knights entered the lists together. Drawing apart, they then rushed furiously at each other, and gave such mighty strokes with the blades of their great swords that their horses were borne to the ground beneath them. Sir Raoul was wounded lightly in the left side; Sir Robert, getting to his feet first, smote him next upon the helm. So powerful was the blow that the sword sheared clear through the helmet to the coif of steel. Sir Raoul staggered; but being a stout champion, he then struck Sir Robert fiercely upon the headpiece, the sword glancing downward to the shoulder and hacking off the mail of the hauberk. Sir Robert, all stunned but not hurt, smote him with all his strength and carried away a quarter of his foe's shield. Wishing himself on a pilgrimage beyond the sea or Robert on his own lands again, Sir Raoul put forward his entire prowess and pressed him grimly; his sword clove to the boss of the shield. For his part, Sir Robert then struck fairly at Sir Raoul, knocking him down. But Raoul, a valiant man who had often ridden with the spears, climbed to his feet in a trice.

Now the two knights fought hand to hand, their armor hewn to pieces and the blood running from their bodies. The fear of death or shame was before their eyes. Sir Robert gripped his sword in both hands and hit his opponent once more upon the helm. Half of it fell asunder. The sword cut through the coif, making a grisly wound. Sir Raoul was beaten to his knees; but he rose immediately and ran at Robert and smote at the remnants of his shield. The thrusts went deep. Coming full upon true armorer's work, however, the sword broke in pieces. When he saw the shards of his sword, Raoul much doubted his victory. He then seized a great stone and flung it at Robert. Sir Robert easily avoided the missile. His adversary turned his back to flee about the lists. So Sir Robert cried that unless his foe admitted himself recreant he would slay him on the spot.

"Gentle knight," Sir Raoul answered. "I yield thee what remains of my sword and throw myself upon thy grace. Spare my life. Take back your land and take my own; for I said naught but foul lies about that fair lady."

When Sir Robert heard this he thought that Raoul might do no more. He urged his lord to pardon him for his crime. His lord agreed to do so, on condition that Raoul should leave his kingdom, never to return.

But Sir Robert found little comfort in this thing because of grief for the faithful lady from whom he had parted, and in no way likewise could he forget John, who was lost to him as well. His lord too shared in his sorrow.

When Madame Jean heard that her husband was victorious she arrayed herself in the richest gown, banded with fine Arabian gold, and was content. So shapely was she, so ravishing, that her very cousin marveled at her beauty.

"Fair cousin," Jean said, "go straight to my father and tell him that his daughter is sound and well. Tell him that if he comes with you, he shall see her with his own eyes. Then lead him here."

The maid did as she was bidden. Going after the damsel, the lord of the castle found his daughter in her chamber. When he saw her face he cast his arms about her neck, shedding tears of joy. Finally, he was able to speak and he asked her where she had been for so long.

"Father, you shall hear of it in due time. But for the love of God, cause my mother to come to me speedily; I die till I see her once again."

Her mother came and, seeing the face she knew so well, fell down in a swoon. While daughter and mother were holding each other fast, the lord went to find Sir Robert. Meeting him, he said:

"Sweet son, very good news have I to share with you."

"Sir, of good news I have great need. Sad at heart am I for the loss of my wife and for the loss of my squire, John."

"Sir Robert, do not pine for John; squires can be found at every turning. But as for your wife, I come from her now; know that she is alive and well."

"Ah, sir," said Robert trembling, "bring me to see that this is true."

"Right willingly."

As soon as Sir Robert saw his wife he ran to her with open arms and embraced her. They kissed each other with many little kisses. Yea, they held each other in this fashion while a man might run ten acres of land, nor did they cease enlacing. The lord commanded that the tables should be spread for supper, and they all ate with mirth and merriment.

After supper they went to their beds; there Sir Robert and his lady talked of many matters. At last he asked her where she had been so great a time.

"Husband, it's a long story; you shall hear of it at a more convenient season. Tell me what you have done all the while."

So he told her the tale she knew by rote, the tale about John his squire who had gained him his bread. So distressed was he over the loss of his companion that on the morrow he would saddle horse and search until he found him.

"Husband, are you set on leaving me again? What shall I do?"

"Lady, I can do none other. Never did a man do such things for a friend as he has done for me. If only you had known him!"

"Truly, I know him well. Nothing of what he did was hid from me."

"Lady, I marvel at such words."

"Sir," she said, "there is no need to wonder. Believe then what I am about to tell you; know assuredly that I am the John whom you would seek. This is how it happened: when I learned of the wager and the outcome and that you had fled because of my faithlessness, I arrayed myself in the guise of a squire and followed you to Paris. From there we journeyed to Marseilles, where I served you as my own liege lord for seven years; nor did I grudge you a valet's service. And know for truth that I am innocent of the foul deed that knight fastened upon me."

Having said thus, Madame Jean embraced Sir Robert and kissed him very sweetly on the mouth. Sir Robert was persuaded that she was John, his squire, and marveled that so high a lady could prove so lowly and so service-able. For which thing he loved her the more dearly all the days of his life.

Thus came together these two parted lovers; thus, on their own domain, which was both broad and rich, they lived a happy life, as becometh lovers in their youth. Often Sir Robert rode to tournaments, and much honor he gained, and wealth. His lands grew to be twice as great. After the death of the father and mother of Lady Jean he was the heir to all their lands. So stout a knight was he that he was made a double banneret and his worth exceeded four thousand pounds. Here ends the story of Sir Robert and his fair lady, Madame Jean.

# The Story of Merlin

*Perhaps the best remembered character from medieval literature,
Merlin appears in countless works of the period. This history of the
wizard's birth and ultimate enchantment is from an anonymous,
15th century French* Roman de Merlin.

hen Constaunce, king of Britain, who had freed the people
from their enemies on all sides, was dead, his eldest son
was taken from the cloister at Winchester, and placed upon
the throne. He was called Moyne the Monk because of his
years in the cloister. Seeing that the new king was unskilled
in the ways of war, Angys, king of Denmark, raised a great army of Danes
and Saxons and sailed for England in many ships.

King Moyne turned to Fortager, who had been his father's steward and
commander of arms, to lead the army against Angys, but Fortager feigned
sickness and refused to go into battle. Moyne led the Britons himself and,
being a novice in the field, lost the battle and a great part of his army, leaving
Angys well fortified in the towns and castles he had captured. Twelve British
Kings who had fought with King Moyne were angry at the loss of the battle
and their men. "Had Fortager led us in battle this would never have happened," they said. "This gabbling monk Moyne is no king for us." These
kings went to Fortager to seek his counsel. "Look to your king for counsel,"
he replied. "Ask for mine only when Moyne is king no longer." Hearing this,
the twelve went straight to Moyne's chambers and slew him while he was at
table. They returned and greeted Fortager, making him their king.

There were many who loved still the race of old King Constaunce, and some faithful barons took the two young princes, brothers of King Moyne, Aurilisbrosias and Uther-Pendragon, and sent them into Brittany lest Fortager should slay them also.

Fortager gathered together all the British kings, and fought a great battle against Angys, and drove him to his ships, and would have killed him on the strand; but Angys sued for peace and made a treaty with King Fortager to make war on him no more. So Angys sailed away with all the remnants of his host, and Fortager marched home in triumph. While he made a feast, there came to him the twelve kings who slew King Moyne, seeking reward, saying, "O King Fortager, behold we have placed thee on high and made thee king; wherefore give us now our meed." Fortager answered, "Being king, in sooth I will show how kings do punish treason": he had wild horses brought and tore the traitors limb from limb upon his castle pavement and nailed their mangled bodies on his walls.

Fortager, with these acts, kindled against himself the wrath of all who had helped to bring him to the throne, and they rose up and joined with those who spoke of bringing back Aurilisbrosias and Uther-Pendragon, and very few still held to Fortager; so he was hunted through his kingdom, and barely escaped with his life. Then he thought to send for Angys in Denmark, and promised him half the kingdom if he would come and help him fight his enemies. And Angys came over again with many men and ships and helped Fortager to fight against the Britons till the people were subdued, kept down by force of sword and spear. So war ceased, but peace never came.

Fortager lived in daily fear of his life; first from the Britons he had betrayed; next from Angys, who, beholding half the kingdom, might seize the whole at any time; and lastly from the Normans, who were like to appear any day to fight for Aurilisbrosias and Uther-Pendragon, to restore them to the throne of their father, Constaunce. To protect himself from all of these, Fortager thought to build a huge castle made of well-hewn stone and timber, a mighty fortress with lofty tower and battlements, deep ditches and a heavy drawbridge, of strength and bigness that the world had never seen. He would build it on the bleak waste of Salisbury Plain, and so dwell safe among his enemies.

Three thousand men began the work at break of day: hewers of wood and carpenters and masons and those who wrought in carved stone. They began to dig out the foundations and lay the mighty blocks well clamped with iron bonds; and when night came they left the ponderous wall reared up breast-high. Next morning, coming to their task, they marveled to find the great stones scattered up and down upon the ground, and all their work destroyed. They worked another day and built the wall up as before, digging the foundations deeper still, and taking greater care to mix the mortar well and fit each stone and clamp it tight. But in the night the wall was once again overthrown, by what power none could tell.

Fortager called ten wise and learned men, and shut them in a chamber open to the sky, to read the stars and divine why no man might build this castle wall. After nine days the wise men came to the king and said: "Sir, we have seen signs in the firmament how an elf-child has been born in Britain, knowing things past and things to come. Find the child and slay him on the plain, and mix the mortar with his blood, and the wall shall stand fast."

Fortager sent men to journey three by three into all parts of the country to seek the child. After wandering many weeks, one of these parties came to a town, where, in the market-place, some children at play were quarreling in their game. "Thou black elf's son," the urchins said to one young playmate five years old, "we will not play with thee, for what thou art we cannot tell." The messengers hearing these words thought this must surely be the child they sought, but Merlin (for it was he) did not leave them long in doubt. "Welcome, O messengers," said he, "behold him whom you seek, yet my blood will never make Fortager's castle wall stand firm for all the wise men say; they are blind fools, who grope among the stars for secrets and blunder the portents at their feet." Hearing this the men wondered greatly, saying "How knowest thou of our errand or of the king's intent?" Merlin answered, "Pictures pass before my mind of all the things that are and shall be. I will go with you to Fortager and show what hinders building his fortress on the plain." So he set out with the messengers, they on their horses, he upon a palfrey.

Now as they journeyed through a town they saw a man buy strong new shoes and leather with which to mend them when worn out: and Merlin

laughed. "Why do you laugh?" the messengers asked. He answered, "Because the man will never wear the shoes." And sure enough he fell dead at his wicket gate. Next day they passed a bier whereon was a child being carried to burial, and a priest sang at the head, and an old man followed behind and wept; and Merlin laughed again, for he said, "Did they but know whose son lies there, the priest would weep and the man would sing." And they found this true, for the lad was not the mourner's son but the priest's. On the third day as they rode, Merlin laughed again, and being asked why, he answered, "King Fortager in his palace is jealous of his wife's handsome chamberlain and threatens to take his life; forsooth he knows not that this good-looking servant is but a woman in disguise." When they came to the palace they found it even as the child had said. Merlin revealed the truth to the king, and the chamberlain was spared.

Fortager marveled much at the wisdom of this child of five years, and talked with him about the mystery of his castle wall and why it was destroyed each night. Merlin said, "The fiends deceived your wise men, showing false signs among the stars; for all my kindred in the air are angry with me because I am baptized into Christendom, and so they try to trick me out of life. They care not for your castle wall, but only for my death. But send men now to dig but a yard beneath the wall's foundation; they shall find swift running water and, underneath, two mighty stones that keep two dragons prisoner. Every night at sundown these two dragons wake and do battle underground, so that the earth quakes and trembles and the wall is shaken down."

Straightway Fortager set his men to dig and find if this was true. They soon came to the stream, which ran both deep and furiously. They made a channel lined with masonry and led the water off another way. And in the river bed were two heavy slabs of stone which it took many men to rear up: and there beneath them lay the dragons. One was red as flame, with eyes that sparkled like the glint from off a brazen helm, his body a full eight yards long and his tail very great and supple. The other one, milk-white and stern of look, had two fierce grisly heads which darted and spat fire white as lightning forks. And as the dragons waked from their slumber, all the men fled away quickly in a panic, save Merlin. Hissing from their dens the two monsters closed in such deadly combat that the air was full of the fire they

belched forth from their throats, the very clouds lightened to the thunder of
the battle, and the earth shook. Thus they fought all that long summer night
with fang and claw and tail; they fell and rose again and rose and fell, nor
flagged neither till the day dawned. Then the red dragon drove the white into
a valley where for a time he stood at bay, until recovering strength he made a
fierce onset, forcing the red dragon back onto the plain again, where fixing
him by the gullet, he smote him down with his white hot flames, scorching
the red dragon to a heap of ashes on the heath. The white dragon flew away
through the air.

After this, Merlin grew in great favor with King Fortager, and was his
counselor in all things that he undertook. The wall no longer fell down as
before. In due time they built the fortress on the plain, a mighty castle high
and strong, of timber and of stone, ramparted on every hand: a fair white
castle the like whereof the world had never seen.

When it was done, men came to Fortager and prayed him ask Merlin what
the battle of the dragons signified.

So Fortager called Merlin, asking whether this battle was a portent of
what might come in the future, but Merlin kept silent. Enraged, Fortager
threatened to slay him if he did not speak.

Merlin smiled in scorn, saying, "You will never see my death-day; nay, if
you bound me fast and drew your sword to strike, you would only fight the
air." Then Fortager entreated him, and swore upon the holy books that no
harm should come to him, whatever the interpretation of the mystery might
be. Then said Merlin, "Hearken to the reading of the portent. The red dragon
so strong to fight represents Fortager and all the power he has gained through
his killing of Moyne the king; the white dragon with two heads stands for
Constaunce's rightful heirs, Aurilisbrosias and Uther-Pendragon, whose
kingdom you withold from them. And, as the white dragon, hunted to the
valley, then regained his strength and drove the red dragon back to the plain,
it means that these heirs whom you have driven to Brittany have there
found help and support and even now sail for this place with many thousand
men, who will come and hunt you through the land till you are driven to
your fortress on the plain, shut up inside therein, and there, with your wife
and child will be burnt to ashes."

Fortager beseeched Merlin to tell him of some way he could avoid this fate, or, at the least, save his own life. Merlin only answered sternly "What will be, will be." When Fortager in his anger went to grasp the seer, Merlin suddenly vanished from sight. Fortager ordered the palace searched high and low, but all the time Merlin was safe and far away in the cell of Blaise the holy hermit. There he remained for a long time, and wrote a book of prophecies of all the things to happen yet in Britain.

As for Fortager it all came to pass as Merlin had foretold, for Uther-Pendragon with his brother Aurilisbrosias landed with an army and marched to Winchester, and the citizens seeing the old banner of their own British kings, overpowered the Danish garrison and threw the gates wide open for the sons of King Constaunce. When Fortager and Angys came against them with a host of Danes and Britons, the Britons of their army refused to fight against their brethren, but rose into revolt. So Aurilisbrosias and Uther-Pendragon won an easy victory and pursued Fortager as far as Salisbury Plain, where he took refuge in his castle. The Britons threw wildfire upon the walls and burned him there, together with his wife and child, and leveled the fortress to the ground.

Angys fled into a citadel and Uther-Pendragon followed, besieging him strongly, but he could not take the place since it was stongly bulwarked and upon a hill. Hearing some barons that had been with Fortager speak oftentimes of Merlin and his exceeding craft, Uther-Pendragon sent out men to search for him. One day while these messengers were at their dinner, an old beggar-man with a long white beard and ragged shoes, and a staff within his hand, came in and asked for alms. They jeered at him bidding him begone. "Wise messengers are ye," the old man said, "that seek the child Merlin, for you have met him often on the road today, and you knew him not. Go home to Uther-Pendragon and say that Merlin awaits him in the wood hard by; for truly none of you will ever find him." And as he spoke these words the old man suddenly vanished. Scarcely knowing whether or not it was a dream, the messengers returned to Uther-Pendragon, who, hearing this, left Aurilisbrosias to continue the siege while he went to the wood to seek Merlin. First a swineherd met him, next a peddler with his pack, each of whom spoke of Merlin; and last there came a comely squire who bade him to wait on, since Merlin was sure to keep the tryst, but had first some work to do. So the prince waited until far into the night and then he saw the squire again, who greeted him saying, "I am Merlin; I will go with you to the camp." When they got there Aurilisbrosias said, "Brother, there came a squire in the night who waked me, saying, 'Behold Angys is come out from his citadel and has stolen past your sentinels, seeking to take your life.' Then I leapt up, and seeing Angys at the tent door I fell on him and slayed him easily, for while the youth stood by I seemed to have the strength of ten, and my sword cut through the brass and iron mail as though they were nothing. As for the squire, I could not find him when the fight was over."

Uther-Pendragon answered, "Brother, the youth was Merlin, who is here with me." At this Aurilisbrosias was very glad, and both the princes thanked Merlin for his help. In the morning when they knew that their leader had been slain, the Danes and Saxons yielded up the castle, asking only for their lives and for leave to sail away in peace to their own country. Thus the land was free again, and all the people took the elder of the brothers, Uther-Pendragon, and made him king in Winchester, and held a coronation feast for a full seven nights.

After this, Merlin told the brothers that one of them would fall in a battle with a very great host of Danes that would come to avenge the death of Angys, yet would he not say which of them it should be. And in a little time the sea about the Bristol Channel was blackened with a multitude of crested ships, and Danes and Saxons swarmed upon the beach in numbers like the sands. Merlin divided the Britons into two companies, so that with one Uther-Pendragon might give battle from the front and draw them inland, whilst Aurilisbrosias with the other stole round between the Northmen and the sea and fought them from the rear. The battle was fierce and bloody before the Britons drove their foes to their ships. Of thirty thousand Danes and Saxons only five thousand went back, and Aurilisbrosias lay dead upon the beach, and with him fourteen thousand Britons, while on the battle-ground for a space three miles by two no man might walk without stepping upon the dead. Merlin made a tomb for Aurilisbrosias with huge stones which he brought from Ireland through the air by magic, and all the people mourned for him.

For seven years after this Uther-Pendragon reigned and prospered, and conquered lands in Normandy and Brittany and Gaul, and Merlin counseled him in all things which he did. Merlin also made for him the famed Round Table where the best and bravest knights might gather in equal seat. One place alone was kept vacant, where none might sit except him who should one day find the Holy Grail.

All came to pass as Merlin had foreseen: when Uther-Pendragon was dead, his son Arthur was chosen king when he had drawn the great sword which was fixed into the stone. Merlin aided Arthur against all his enemies, and saved him from many perils which threatened his life. But at length the time drew nigh when Merlin should no more sojourn among men.

And it came to pass that Merlin made a wondrous tomb in the Church of St. Stephen at Camelot for twelve kings which Arthur slew. He made twelve images of bronze overlaid with gold, and a figure of King Arthur raised above with his sword drawn in his hand. Each image bore a waxen taper which burned day and night. And Merlin told the king, "By these you will know when I pass from the world of living men. On that day the tapers will go out and will never after be rekindled. For you there remains a life of glory. The search for the Holy Grail shall be achieved, and you shall pass almost within its presence, yet not see it with your eyes, since they have looked too much upon the blood and dust of war to be shown the marvel of that holy thing. Fighting will never cease in your day, but you shall gain the victory and be king of Christendom, and at last die nobly in battle as a king should die. But for me, alas! I must be imprisoned in the air alive, and wait through the ages for my judge, awake through all the weary years, while others sleep beneath in quiet ground."

Then Arthur advised him, since he knew his fate, to guard himself against it by his subtle arts. But the seer answered, "That which shall be is; it is as unchangeable as that which was."

In the years that passed, the spirits of the air sought every opportunity to trap him and snatch him from the earth: but Merlin, knowing their plans, defeated them at every turn and was able to complete his work. But as he waxed in years he was beguiled by a beautiful damsel of the lake, called Niniame, and he fell into a dotage for love of her and would follow her wherever she went. But Niniame became weary of his love, made sport of him, and only endured his company for the wonders that he showed her. And one day as they sat together in a wood at Broceliande, she entreated Merlin to teach her a certain powerful spell, where a man might be shut up forever in a narrow space about the earth, walled in by air, invisible to all forevermore. She begged with tears and promised him her love if he would show it her. And when she tired him with her asking, and cajoled him with many sweet words, he showed her what she asked. Then Niniame lulled him to sleep upon her lap, and rising softly, wrought the spell in the air; and so shut Merlin up forever in a blackthorn tree within the lonesome wood at Broceliande, where his spirit, tangled in a hopeless maze among the weird black twigs, becomes more and more entangled as it struggles to get free, even to this day.

# The Cursed Dancers of Colbek

*An extended anecdote illustrating the pitfalls of pronouncing curses on others, this bizarre story is from Robert of Brunne's* Handlyng Synne.

ancing, singing, and similar frolicking games — whoever frequently partakes of such shameful revels in churches or in churchyards should fear the price of sacrilege. All such things are forbidden while the priest presides over mass. Acting out farces, playing the pipe, or beating the tambourine while the congregation prays or listens to the sermon will enrage any priest even more than the talk of fools or heretics.

Speaking of dancing during church, I shall tell to you now the story of a terrible fate, and by my honor the tale I will unfold is true as Gospel. This tale took place in a land called England, during the reign of Edward the king.

It happened on a Christmas Eve. Twelve revelers, dancing arm in arm, singing with frenzy and madness, came to a town called Colbek. The dancers appeared at the town church, which was named after Saint Magne the martyr. The group was led by a man named Gerlew, and it was he who inspired the dancers to their frenzy. They came to Colbek, the story goes, for a simple reason: to enlist in their troupe a girl named Ave, the daughter of the town priest. As well as his daughter, the priest had a son, whom everyone knew as Azone. Each of the dancers consented to the will of the leader, Gerlew, who wondered aloud who among them could best entice the priest's daughter into joining them in their wild revels. There were two maidens among the dancers, and it took but little time for Gerlew to send them, Bessyne and Melinde, to tempt the poor young Ave. The two women went and enticed Ave to join them in their caroling in the churchyard. As soon as the girl joined them, Gerlew taught her their song: "Why do we stand here? Why shouldn't we go on?" They danced and sang without fear of their folly, reveling all the time through twilight and the close of matins, singing madly even through vespers. Ave's father, the priest, donned his holy vestments and went up to the altar, ready to begin mass. But the dancers refused to stop, even as the priest raised prayers, and suddenly, furious at the commotion in the churchyard, the priest rushed out onto the church steps. He cried at the dancers: "On God's behalf, I forbid you to continue these shameful revels, and command you to enter my church and pray, as is proper on Christ's own birthday."

Despite his commands, the dancers continued their frenzied song, swirling in each other's arms. Enraged, the priest prayed to God and Saint Magné, the patron of his church, that in punishment for their disrespect the dancers not be able to stop their shameful revels until a year had passed. No sooner had the priest spoken than each of the dancers' hands became locked in the hands of their partners, and so strongly and firmly that for the next twelve months no one could break them apart. The priest went back into the church and asked his son, Azone, to go among the dancers and bring his daughter, Ave, into the church, but it was too late. His curse had fallen upon his daughter as well as the other dancers. With great speed Azone went into the circle of dancers and pulled and pulled on his sister's arm, trying to free her from her partners. He pulled so hard that her arm finally came loose from her body, and everyone marveled that, like a branch snapped off of its tree, neither the arm nor the shoulder shed a drop of blood, cold or hot. Azone returned to his father with the grisly present and cried aloud, "Here is the arm of my sister and your daughter, whom I tried to save. Your curse has taken vengeance on your own flesh and blood; you cursed too strongly and too soon; you wanted vengeance and here is the answer to your prayer."

You need not imagine the sorrow of the priest, nor will I try to describe it. He took his daughter's arm and buried it the next morning, but the following morning Ave's arm was found lying above the grave. The priest tried burying the arm twice more, and each morning the ground gave it back up, refusing to contain it. Burdened by the terrible curse, he carried the arm into the church so all could see it.

Meanwhile, the revelers were still bound hand in hand, dancing round and round in the very spot where they had been cursed. They felt no fatigue, neither ate nor drank, never took so much as a wink of sleep, as night and day they danced on and on. Frost or snow, they felt no cold; rain or sleet they felt no pain. All who saw them marveled that their hair never grew nor their fingernails, that their clothes never grew dirty or ragged, and that thunder and lightning did them no harm. They never changed, but sang their song: "Why do we stand here? Why shouldn't we go on?"

Is there anyone alive who would not go to see such a miracle? The emperor came from Rome to witness this hard fate, and he wept with pity at the dancers' plight. The emperor called for carpenters to build a shelter above the dancers to protect them from the elements, but each morning all that they had built was found torn asunder. It was clear that nothing could be done until the year of the curse had passed.

Twelve months passed, and on Christmas Eve, at the very hour the curse had been pronounced, they flew apart and fled into the church, where they fell to the floor as if dead. For three days none of the dancers stirred, their flesh and bones lay still as dust, but on the third day they rose and spoke as one to the priest: "You are the cause of our long confusion, the author of our long grief, which so many have come to marvel at. But your own confusions will end very soon, for you'll shortly be off to your eternal reward."

All of the dancers had risen together and spoken those words except Ave, who lay dead.

Though he didn't fear death, the priest was the first in town to die after his daughter. For Ave's arm that wouldn't lie still in the grave, the emperor ordered a special vessel made to contain it. He ordered it hung in the church so all could see it and think about the curse that caused it.

The revelers who had danced the whole year, bound hand in hand, never came together again, except in their thoughts when they heard their story told, as it was throughout the world. Many of them went to Rome, though they went separately, never meeting. Their clothes never got dirty, their fingernails never grew, and their hair never changed color. I heard it told that they never found any cure at any holy shrine.

This tale illustrates plainly the folly of pronouncing curses, and I've told it to you to make you afraid of reveling in a church or a churchyard, or against a priest's will, to dance when he tells you to be still.

# Palamon and Arcite

*This story, Chaucer's Knight's Tale, follows Boccaccio's Tesieda much more closely than the classical sources that Chaucer credits. Despite his debt to the Italian, the style and flavor are uniquely Chaucer's.*

 nce, the old stories tell us, there was a king named Theseus, who was lord and governor of Athens. In his time there was no greater conqueror, for he had taken the land of the Amazons, which was called Scythia, had married their queen Hippolyta and brought her back to Athens with him, accompanied by her fair sister Emily. Of course, if it were not too long to tell here I would tell you of how the battle was won, of the great fight between the men of Athens and the Amazons, how the fair Queen Hippolyta was conquered, of the feast at their wedding, and their return to Athens and the storm that greeted them, but I must forbear to tell this part of the tale, as my part is long enough . . . and I'll leave that story to another.

As Theseus and his retinue approached Athens, he noticed a company of women all in black. Two by two they knelt at the side of the road and raised such cries of woe as had never been heard by any living creature. They did not cease their cries till they had seized Theseus's bridle. He said to them, "Who are you that disturb the day of my homecoming and my happiness with your wails? Is it envy of my honors that makes you cry so? Or has someone really mistreated or offended you? Tell me if your sorrow can be amended, and why it is that you are dressed in black."

The eldest of the women, started to speak and fell into a swoon that was almost as death. When she recovered she said, "My Lord, who has been granted this victory and whom fortune gives the life of a conqueror, we do not begrudge you your victory or your honor, but beg for your mercy and your help. We have waited for you here this entire fortnight, help us now with your great might."

"For sure my lord, there is not one of us here that has not been a duchess or a queen. I, the wretch that speaks to you now, was the wife of King Cappaneus, who was killed at Thebes — cursed be that day! Each of us here before you lost our husbands in that siege and old King Creon, who rules over Thebes, not satisfied with victory, in anger and in spite, refused our husbands both burial or burning, and left their bodies piled outside the city for the dogs."

Theseus, his stern demeanor vanished, was filled with pity and felt that his heart would break for these poor women, so recently of good estate. He drew them to their feet and swore, as he was a good knight, to avenge them on the tyrant Creon, saying that all in Greece would know that it was a death well-deserved.

He waited not even half a day, nor did he enter the city, but sent Hippolyta and Emily ahead to Athens to wait for his return. He unfurled his proud banner, white and all worked in gold, bold Mars in red with spear and shield, and the image of the minotaur he slew in Crete, and headed towards Thebes, his army at his side.

They arrived at Thebes, and to make short work of this thing, quickly did battle with Creon, slew him as a knight should on field of battle, and set his army to flight. They then besieged and won the city, breaking down wall and beam and rafter. To the women he restored the bones of their husbands so they could carry out the proper rites. At the end of that day, after the battle was won, Theseus took his rest on the field of battle while his men despoiled the field, stripping the bodies of harness, weapons and wealth. As they searched they found two young knights, lying side by side, in the same armor, greatly wounded but not quite dead, though not quite alive either. From their arms and devices the heralds knew them to be of royal blood and sons of two sisters of Thebes. They carried them gently to the tent of

Theseus, who had them sent to Athens to dwell in prison for life, with no hope of ransom. Their names were Palamon and Arcite.

Theseus returned home, wearing the laurel of the conqueror, and lived in joy and honor in his court, while above, in a high tower, full of anguish and full of woe, dwelt the two young knights.

So passed year by year and day by day, till one fine morning in the month of May, Emily, fairer than the lily upon its green stalk and fresher than the new flowers, appeared in the garden before the break of day to gather flowers and pay homage to the springtime (for May allows no slugabeds). Her golden hair was gathered in plaited tresses that fell a good yard behind her back and she sang with the voice of an angel as she gathered red and white flowers for a garland. The part of the garden that she walked in was hard by the tower where Palamon and Arcite were imprisoned.

Palamon, as was his habit, with leave of his jailer, rose early and paced the high chamber bemoaning his state to himself, when, by fate or by chance, he spied Emily through the heavy bars. He grew pale and cried out as though pierced through the heart. Arcite started up at his cry and said, "My cousin, what ails you? Why are you so pale? Who has hurt you? For God's love you must be patient that we are in prison, for it will never be anything else. Our fate was sealed by some arrangement of the stars at our birth, and we must endure — that's the long and short of it."

Palamon replied, "Cousin, if you are of that opinion, you have a vain imagination. It is not this prison that makes me cry out and turn pale. The fairness of that lady in the garden is the cause of my woe. I don't know if she's a woman or a goddess, but I believe she is Venus." And, saying this, he fell to his knees praying, "Venus, if it is your will to appear before this poor creature, help us to escape from this prison and, if it is our destiny to die here, look with favor on our line, fallen so low."

As he was praying Arcite spied Emily in the garden and the sight wounded him as much as it had Palamon, if not more so. He sighed and cried out, "The fresh beauty that roams in yonder garden suddenly slays me. Unless I have her mercy and her grace, at least to see her, I am as good as dead."

Palamon, hearing this turned quickly and said, "Do you say this in earnest or in jest?" "Nay," replied Arcite, "in earnest. By my faith, I'm in no mood to jest."

"It will do you no great honor to be false and to betray me." said Palamon. "We are cousins and brothers under oath, sworn to help each other in all things, till death parts us. You should aid me further in my every cause, as I would advance all of yours. I saw her first, and it is your duty to help me. Or prove yourself false."

To this Arcite proudly replied, "You are the one who acts falsely, and I'll tell you why: I loved her first as a real woman. Can you deny that you did not know if you had seen a woman or a goddess? Yours is a spiritual affection, mine is true human passion. But really, it matters little who saw her first, for, as the wise men say 'Who can give a lover any law?' Love is a law that is greater than any given to man. She may be a maid or a widow or a wife; and it's not likely that in our whole lives you or I will ever stand in her favor. We are both condemned to die in this prison unransomed. Should we be like the two hounds who, while fighting all day over a bone, had it carried away by a kite, and gained nothing? It is every man for himself; you love and so will I, that's all there is to it. In this prison we must endure, that's our fate, you must be sure."

The cousins in their tower lived in great bitterness and strife as the years past. One day, a worthy prince, Pirithous by name, came to Athens. He was a childhood friend of Theseus and they loved each other greatly. This Pirithous had known Arcite well many years ago in Thebes, and through his prayers and pleas Theseus consented to set Arcite free, without ransom, making him swear, on pain of death, never to set foot again into any of his lands.

Arcite sped home to Thebes, to his great sorrow, for now he finds himself in a different sort of prison. "Alas," he lamented, "now my fate is to dwell not in purgatory but in hell. Dear cousin Palamon, yours is the victory: happily you can endure prison. Prison? No, paradise, for fortune has turned your way and you have sight of her while I am exiled here. You are a worthy and able knight, and may, in some way, since fortune always changes, be able to win your desire."

Palamon, seeing Arcite gone, swore so that the great tower resounded with his cries and bitter tears fell upon his fetters. "Ah, cousin Arcite, the fruit of all our strife is yours. You now walk through Thebes a free man. As you are wise and brave you may gather all of our kin and make bold war upon this city, and by some chance or treaty, you may possess the lady for whom I live."

You lovers, here's a question for you: who has had the worst fate, Palamon or Arcite? The one may see his lady daily, but in his tower prison must stay. The other in Thebes rides free, but cannot see the lady of his desire. Choose as you like if you can, I'll continue my tale as I began.

Arcite had been in Thebes for a year or two. In all this time he hardly slept or ate or drank. Thin and dry as chaff, with hollow eye and ashen visage, he was indeed a sorry sight. He spent his time alone, wailing at night, bemoaning his fate, weeping at the sound of music or singing.

One night, as he slept, the winged god Mercury appeared to him, dressed as he had been when he lulled the Argus to sleep. He told Arcite, "You must go to Athens, for there lies the end of your woe." Arcite rose from his bed and said: "How true and right this is. I will go to Athens straightaway; the fear of death shan't stop me if I can but see Emily. Death is no matter."

He saw his face in the mirror and realized that he was so greatly changed from his years of melancholy that, with different costume, he might walk about Athens and see his lady without anyone knowing him. He put on the clothes of a poor laborer and, taking with him one faithful squire, who was in his complete trust and was similarly attired, set off for Athens that same day.

Arcite presented himself at the court as a servant, willing to do whatever they wished and shortly found work with the chamberlain of Emily's house. He was wise and worked hard, for he still had his mighty frame and long bones and did every job well and without complaint. For two years he was in service and became well-loved by all at the court. He called himself Philostratus. His name grew well known, as did his good work and clever tongue, to Theseus, who raised him up to be squire of his own chamber. He was given gold to maintain his station, which he spent wisely with the income smuggled to him from Thebes. Within three years time, there was not another man in all the kingdom, whether in peace or war, whom Theseus trusted more.

But now I return to Palamon, who, in his dark cell has sat these seven long years. It fell in that seventh year, in the beginning of May, whether by chance or by fate, Palamon escaped his prison. With the help of a friend, he administered to his jailer a powerful sleeping draught made of the herbs and opiates of Thebes that made the jailer sleep so soundly none could make him stir. Palamon fled as far as he could, but, it being after midnight and the morning close at hand, he found a grove and thought to spend the day there and to continue on to Thebes that night. His only thought was to return home, gather an army and to make war upon Theseus to gain Emily as his wife; or, in the siege to lose his life.

I turn again to Arcite, now Philostratus, Theseus' squire, who on that same May morning rose up early and, taking a fiery steed, thought to ride a mile or two out of the city to observe the month. As it happened, he came to the very grove where Palamon was hiding and, leaping from his horse, proceeded to lustily sing and gather branches of woodbine for a wreath. Palamon crouched in fear of his life, not knowing his cousin for all the time that had passed. Truly has it been said these many years that the field has eyes and the wood has ears. Men must carry themselves carefully, for chance encounters happen daily.

Arcite had gathered his branches and fell from his song to a deep melancholy. This is the way with lovers; always in sunshine or heavy rain, like a well-bucket, first up then down again.

"A curse upon the day I was born," Arcite mourned, "to be captive and slave of my mortal enemy, serving him as his squire. To further my disgrace, I dare not even use my true name. Once I was Arcite, noble born, now I am called Philostratus, a name worthy of nothing. Oh Mars! Oh Jupiter! You have let our line fall so low! Only I and the wretched Palamon, martyred in prison, are left. More than this, you have let Emily slay me with her eyes. It was my fate, before I ever came to Athens, that she would be my death. All my other troubles are as nothing if only I could win her pleasure."

He fell to musing and Palamon, hearing his speech, recognized his cousin and felt a cold sword slide through his heart. He rose from the thicket, ashen and shaking and cried, "Arcite, false traitor, you are caught, you who love my lady so, cause of all my pain. You are of my blood and to my counsel

sworn, but you've tricked Theseus and falsely changed your name to gain the love of Emily. Though I have no weapon in this place, you will give her up or die. Choose!"

Arcite heard his speech and, pulling out his sword scornfully, replied, "By God! Were you not sick for love and had no weapon, you would not leave this grove alive. I will love Emily despite all you say, but, as you are a noble knight, am willing to decide our fate in battle. I will return to you here tonight with food and drink and bedding and come again in the morning with two sets of weapons. You choose first and leave me the rest, and if it should pass that you slay me in this wood, she is yours."

Arcite did as he promised. They met that morning without salute or "good day," but quickly and quietly armed each other and entered into the fray. Palamon fought like a lion and Arcite, fierce as a tiger, returned his dangerous long spear thrusts. Soon the soil was mired ankle-deep in their blood, but now, I leave them fighting in the grove.

Destiny, minister of the earth, executes the fate that God himself decrees, and though the world may promise the opposite of a thing, it can happen on any given day that which otherwise would never come to pass in a thousand years.

This fate brought Theseus, his queen Hippolyta and the fair Emily out upon the hunt that same morning. Riding for a grove where they had been told there was a great hart, they reached a stand of trees, and, instead of the hart, Theseus spied Arcite and Palamon, fierce as boars in battle, their swords flashing to and fro, their lightest strokes seemingly strong enough to fell an oak.

Theseus charged between them on his courser, and with drawn sword cried "Halt! Not another stroke on pain of losing your heads! Who are you knights who fight here privately, without judge or seconds, but nobly, as in the lists?"

Palamon answered quickly: "Sire, there is little to say. We both deserve death, for we are wretched captives encumbered by our very lives. Slay me first or us both together, but know this: my fellow is your mortal enemy Arcite, who all these many years has pretended to be your squire Philostratus because of his love for the fair Emily. Know this too, that I am Palamon, your mortal foe, escaped from prison for love of Emily. I am happy to die in her sight; execute your judgment on both of us as is only right."

Theseus shouted: "This is indeed a short conclusion — you've damned yourself by your own confession; and you'll have no need to wait, you shall be dead by mighty Mars, and have your fate."

The Queen and Emily began to weep for these knights of noble estate, whose only crime was love, and for their cruel fate. "Have pity on us women, lord," they cried, and, falling to their knees, begged Theseus to spare the two.

Theseus pondered the cousins and their crimes. Though their actions had raised his anger, his reason knew their cause. He relented passing sentence and announced to one and all: "The god of love observes no obstacles, and should well be called the god of miracles! Arcite and Palamon, safely out of prison, could have lived in Thebes royally, but venture here where death is certain. And here is the greatest jest of all: they vie for love of one who knows them not at all!" He said to them, "For the wishes of my Queen kneeling here, and for the tears of Emily, her sister dear, if both of you now truly swear, that nevermore should your country dare, to war on mine in night or day but to be friends in all that may, my pardon now I'll gladly give, and leave you both, brave knights, to live."

Then Theseus said: "For my sister Emily, over whom you've had such strife and jealousy, she cannot well have husbands two, even if both your loves to be true. And so I propose this decree: that you should go forth separately, raise one hundred knights each, return back here when one year is through and let a battle of the lists decide who shall be the husband of this fair bride."

Now who was happier, Palamon or Arcite? Both leapt for joy at Theseus' fair judgement, thanked their lord and made for Thebes as quickly as they could go.

Then Theseus prepared the field royally, cleared the grove for a full mile around and built a theatre of the same size, round like the compass, with stands a full sixty paces tall so all could see the spectacle. No expense was spared and every worthy artisan and stonemason in the country was engaged. Two great gates of white marble stood, one to the East and one to the West, and the arena was crowned by three temples — one to Venus, goddess of love, one to Mars in all his warlike splendor and the third to Diana, goddess of chastity and the hunt. Each temple was a marvel to behold, each full of noble carving and portraiture, the shapes, the contours and the figures were the finest ever made. When at last all was finished at great cost, the temples and the theatre complete in every way, there was little time to wait, for the year had almost passed.

Both Palamon and Arcite arrived with their hundred knights, all brave and strong from many a land, for the right to fight in this contest was the wish of every knight. To fight on a noble field for a great prince, for the love of a fair lady, what could be better?

In Palamon's company was Lycurgas, king of Thrace. Great and black was his beard, manly his face, his eyes glowed yellow and red and he seemed like a gryphon as he looked about, riding in his chariot drawn by four white bulls, clothed not in armor but spiked with yellow nails as bright as gold.

With Arcite came Emertreus, king of India, seated on a saddle of beaten gold astride a bay steed covered by a cloth of gold. His coat was of Tartar fabric, covered with pearls. His voice was a trumpet, and on his hand he carried for his pleasure a lily-white eagle.

Each of the hundred knights carried the weapons they thought best, one with a breastplate another with a coat of mail, one with an iron mace another with an ax or a prussian shield. In all it was the greatest show that was ever on a field.

Before dawn, Palamon went to the temple of Venus to pray, where, on bended knee he said, "Have pity on my bitter tears and part, your mercy on my lover's heart. I do not ask tomorrow to have victory, renoun in this fight or vainglory. I simply want my lady in my arms, and though Mars is the god of arms, your virtue is so sweet in heaven above, that if you wish it, I'll have my love."

Palamon made his sacrifice carefully, and after some pause the statue shook, which he took to be a good omen and went on his way.

Later that morning as the sun rose, so did Emily, who brought herself to Diana's temple, where, with her maidens she offered ritual and sacrifice in proper form, and prayed to the goddess thus: "Oh chaste goddess of the woods green, to whom all in heaven and earth is seen, know that I desire to be a maiden all my life, never would I be a lover or a wife. I but wish to walk in the forest wild, and never to have to be with child. For Palamon and Arcite who have such strife for me, let peace and love once more between them be." Then Diana appeared, spoke to her and said: "Among the gods it is affirmed, and by the eternal, written and confirmed, that thou shalt be wedded to one of those, who for your love has had such woes, but unto which I may not tell. Farewell, for here I may no longer dwell." "Alas," cried Emily, "I place myself in your hands," and sadly went on her way.

The following hour belonged to Mars, and Arcite walked to his temple to make his sacrifice and he prayed: "Oh strong god, and you who hold, for every reign in every land, the bridle of their armies in your hand, I am young and foolish as you know, but am with love afflicted so, that I must have the strength to win her in this place, and well I know I need your help and grace. Without your help my might will not prevail, so help me lord tomorrow, in my travail. If on the field I shall have victory, mine will be the battle, and yours the glory." The doors of the temple banged and the fires burned bright, while sweet smells rose from the ground. The statue of the god began to ring and Arcite thought he heard the word "Victory" and left the temple happy.

As soon as this was done great strife broke out in the heavens between Venus and Mars, and Jupiter tried vainly to settle it till aged Saturn appeared and said to Venus, "Fear not, Palamon who is thy servant shall have his lady as was your covenant. Mars will help his knight to win the day, but this battling between you must stop. I am your ally, ready at your will, weep no more, for your desires I'll fulfill."

In the morning, as the day began to dawn, the sound of horses and harnesses was heard all about the inns. Many lords rode to the palace to see the different costumes and arms, so exotic and rich and made with such expert goldsmithing, embroidery and iron work. Bright shields, golden helmets and coats of arms shone, while armorers rushed to and fro with file and hammer. Sturdy yeomen passed on foot carrying their stout staves, steeds foamed upon golden bridles and the sound of pipes, drums and horns filled the air. Many went through the palace in threes and tens, looking on the strange knights, trying to decide which would put up the best fight.

At last the hour had come and Theseus called the throng to silence and said: "It is foolish now for us to spend, such noble blood in a battle to the end; so to assure they shall not die, I will my first proposal modify. No man now, on pain of loss of life, shall bring to battle shot or ax or knife, nor shall any have a short sword at their side, and no man shall to his fellow ride, except on course and with sharp ground spear; and once on foot, with his longsword may perservere, and he that has fallen shall on no account be slain, but shall be brought to his enemy's stake, and there he must remain. There shall be a stake for either side, and once taken there by force a knight must there abide. And at last, if either chieftain fall, the tourney's over, the fighting's done, and that will be it all."

Theseus and his knights took their place with Hippolyta and Emily, and from the west through the gate of Mars came Arcite with his hundred knights, while at the same moment, from the east Palamon entered at Venus' gate with his men. In all the world there had never been seen such an even match. Neither company seemed to have the other at advantage in worthiness, estate or age. They formed two fair ranks and had their names called aloud so in all their numbers there was no guile, and the gates were shut behind them. The heralds having ridden to and fro fell back and the clarion sounded and the trumpets blew. Lances were set and sharp spurs were put to the sides as east charged west. These were truly knights who could joust and ride! They broke their lances against stout shields, and spears flew twenty feet into the air. Knights, now on the ground, drew sharp swords and with silver blades did hew and rend. With mighty maces they mauled men's bones and bright ribbons of blood flowed all round. Now a steed would stumble and his rider rolls underfoot as does a ball. Another fights with his truncheon, sturdy on the ground unseating another. One knight, wounded through the body sore, is dragged struggling to the stake where he must stay, but soon another lad in on the stake opposed and again the sides are matched. Theseus bade them rest a while and drink and then the tourney started off anew.

Many times that day the two sides met. Each time both sides unhorsed and hurt their fellow knights. No tigress, bereft of her cub, ever fought like Arcite and no hunted lion mad with hunger sought blood as did Palamon. Their jealous strokes their helmets hacked, their sides were all bloody, the end was near. Strong King Emetreus grasped Palamon as he fought with Arcite and struck him a deep blow with his sword, and by the force of twenty strong knights Palamon was dragged, unyielding, towards the stake. In trying to rescue Palamon great King Lycurgas is brought down, and even Emetreus for all his strength is thrown from his saddle by Palamon, before he is taken. His stout heart cannot help him now, and at the stake he must stay.

When Theseus saw this sight he cried, "No more, for it is done. The tourney's over, Arcite has won!" Theseus then turned to the crowd and said "I will be the judge, and I say it fairly, that Arcite has bravely won the hand of Emily."

What can fair Venus do above? What says she now this queen of love? She cries with bitter tears to Saturn, who says "Dear daughter have no fears, for Mars has his will and his knight the day, and by my word, you will have your way."

Their heralds blew their trumpets and Arcite in his triumph removed his helmet and rode the length of the theatre, his eyes fixed on Emily, who returned his look with friendly eye. But out of the ground a fury sprang, sent straight from hell by Pluto and so frightened his steed that it lept back in fear, dashing Arcite to the ground before he could regain his seat. His chest was smashed by his saddle bow, and the blood rushed to his face which turned a deadly black. He was carried from the field and laid in bed at the palace, where his armor was cut off and all manner of physicians ministered to him. He was still alive, with sound mind and memory, and cried out over and over again for Emily.

The days passed and their hopes passed with them, for it was clear that nothing the doctors could do would help him. And so he called at last for Emily and for Palamon, and when they drew near he said to Emily, "I placed you in this world on high, o'er every creature, and now I die. Alas the woe, the pain is strong, and I have suffered for you long! Now gently take me in your arms, I pray, and for the love of God, listen well to what I say. I have had here with my cousin Palamon great strife and anger, which is now all gone. In all the world there is not one so worthy to be loved as Palamon. He serves you now, and will all your life. Think of him should you become a wife." The cold of death crept up to his chest, and his strength flowed out till none was left. His eyes clouded over, and with his last breath, he whispered, "Emily!"

Great was the sorrow throughout the land at the news of his death. Such weeping was not seen at Troy when Hector was carried home. In the grove where Palamon and Arcite first fought Theseus built a great bier made of oak and trees of every description. Many were the nymphs and fauns that were driven from their homes as the trees fell all around.

The streets of Athens were draped in black and Arcite, on the shoulders of the most noble Athenians, was carried slowly up the hill. Theseus and his father Aegeus followed next, then Palamon and Emily after. The pyre was high and burned for hours, and the noble Greeks cast milk, honey and blood into the fire; some threw their weapons or their jewels. The knights, as is the custom, rode around the pyre, keeping it to their left, shouting and making three circles. Spears clanged and women wailed, and after the ashes were cold the wake was kept the whole night.

Time passed and, in the natural order of things, mourning was forgotten. Theseus called Emily to him, and summoned Palamon, who did not know the reason and appeared still in his black mourning clothes. Theseus drew them together and said, "It is wisdom, it seems to me, to make virtue of necessity, and to take well that which we cannot eschew, for frankly it is our common due. Whoever grumbles is but a fool, and takes exception to the world's great rule. Certainly a man is most in his honor, to die in his excellence and in flower. It is truly best for worthy fame to die when one is in the best of name. The contrary of this is madness. Why do we grumble? Why all this sadness? Arcite, the flower of chivalry, departed from us in honor and bravery; he has escaped the prison of this life, so why are downcast here his cousin and his wife? For his welfare, who loved them so well, can he thank them? Only Jove can tell! The point of this long argument is that woe should turn to merriment, and thank the gods for all their grace and ere before we leave this place. Sister," he said, "it is my full intent with all the Ayes' of this parliament, that gentle Palamon, your own knight, who serves you with full heart and might, who ever since he knew your face has longed for you to share his grace, shall be taken as your husband and your lord. Lend me your hand if we are in accord." To Palamon he turned and said, "I trust I need little persuasion to gain your consent on this occasion."

They were married soon amidst the assembled lords, and finally with bliss and with song, gentle Palamon was united with Emily. God granted him the love he so dearly bought, and Emily loved him tenderly and he served her so gently, that never between them came harsh words or jealousy.

So ends the tale of Palamon and Emily, God bless all of this fair company!

# Sir Gawain and the Green Knight

*Fantastic, lyrical and allegorical, Sir Gawain's insistence on honor and courage, even when it necessitates avoiding love and facing certain death, remains perhaps the most famous of Arthurian legends.*

ince the siege was ceased at Troy, the buildings broken and burned to ashes, the man who played the tricks of treason there was tried for all his treachery, the truest in the world. The Trojans, fleeing, scattered all across the earth, founded kingdoms, laid down new roots. Bold Brutus wandered over banks both broad and steep, and joyously founded Britain. Where war and wrath and wonder, have existed since within; and to bold knights bliss and blunder, offered grace and offered sin.

More fabulous tales unfolded on the fields of Britain than on any I've ever known. And of all the fables that I have heard, of all the stories I've stayed awake studying, the most fantastic happened in the court of King Arthur, the noblest leader of the land. And I shall relate to you a true adventure, which many have marked wonderful to hear — a tale of courage even for Arthur's courageous court. And if you will listen but a little while, I shall tell it at once, as I once heard it told. I'll tell it as it's said and spoken, this story swift and strong; tell it in rhymes that shan't be broken, this tale both brief and long.

'Twas Christmas, and King Arthur lay at Camelot with many lovely knights and ladies of the best. There in the spirit of the great Round Table they rose to revels high with myriad mirths. The gentle knights there jousted and carole dances came to mark a feast that lasted fifteen days, a feast filled full with all the meat and merriment good men could make. But Arthur would not eat until all were served. With a pleasure in life that men still praise, his young blood busy and his brave brain wild, he insisted on hearing a strange story before anyone ate — a marvelous tale he could believe as true. Therefore, his subjects near, he beckoned with a call; saying that before New Year, a story should be told them all.

No sooner had the king asked for a story than strange and strident sounds filled the great hall, and through its arched doors an ugly giant came. From his chest to his calves — both as thick as those of any knight — he seemed a gruesome giant. They wondered at his color, this giant man and mean; and fell silent to each other, amazed that he was green.

The knight was green and so was all he wore. His cloak, the finest ever seen, was of green silk, embroidered with emeralds sewn with golden threads. And the stockings and tunic, his shield and his pointed boots were green as grass. The beast he rode was green as he: A huge green steed, neighing restless under saddle; a horse to lead, bold knights into bolder battle.

The green knight's beard fell like bushes on his chest, and lengthy locks fell like leaves on strong, straight shoulders. The horse's mane was green as the giant's hair, and curled and combed and tied in careful knots. But the green knight carried no weapons of war, no hefty hauberk, spiked spurs or shining spear. He held in one hand a branch of holly, a green branch even while others are bare, and his other hand held a tall, thick axe. It had a head as big as a sheep and bright green tassels all along its shaft. He rode up to the table, daring any to bar his way; and said "Is the king here able, to listen to what I say?"

The knights and ladies at the table whispered, "Who is this green knight, what is his game?" King Arthur rose up straight and said, "Noble knight, my name is King Arthur and I rule this castle. You're welcome to this feast and all we have." The giant answered, "No, heaven help me if I come here for your food. I have no time for that. My errand is not to share your songs or lounge with these fair ladies. All shout your praises to the sky, King Arthur, and the praises of your barons, the best and the boldest most men say. I've come to test your courage — have no fear, this holly branch proves that I come in peace. But if you are as brave and bold as bright men say, grant me a little game this holiday." King Arthur answered fast, saying, "Sir, courteous knight, this court's glory hasn't passed, if you want you'll get a fight."

"No, I don't ask to fight," the green knight said, "the beardless boys before me wouldn't stand a chance waging war with me. But it's the last day of the year, and I ask to be granted a gentle game. If there be any who holds himself hardy here, bold in his blood, let him come quick and strike me a stroke with this axe. I will stand it in my stead, stiff and still. But then I will swing my steel at he who strikes at me. A blow for a blow. But I'll give him the respite, of a twelvemonth and a day; as you have heard me right, now what have you to say?"

Though he silenced them at first, stiller were they then, when with wide eyes and green brows furrowed he told them all his game. When no one spoke, he said, "Ho, ho: is this brave Arthur's court, the renowned Round Table? No man here makes me marvel." Angry, Arthur advanced, while the green knight stood his ground. "Your fun is foolish and your game more weary than wise. But you'll find more than your match here, sir." Arthur grabbed the great axe and swung it in his stride, as the green knight dismounted in a second and stood still staring. To stand a stroke or drink a draught of wine seemed all the same to him. Then, from beside the Queen, Sir Gawain stood suddenly and tall; saying, "King Arthur I am keen, to match this green man in our hall."

Sir Gawain came forward and King Arthur said, "Keep thee careful, cousin, and with this weapon deal this green knight what he desires. If you strike strong and sure, you needn't fear this green man in a year." With axe in hand, Gawain greeted the green knight, granted him a bow and heard the giant's words: "Repeat to me, Gawain, before we further go, what is our game. Try no tricks on me: you lose should I not trust you." "I'm to strike a blow at you," said gallant Gawain, "and a twelfthmonth hence, ye shall strike at me — you and no other." The green knight said, "Gawain, I see that you're the man; who for honor risks great pain, as the truly noble can."

"Where will I find you New Year next, for I know not your name nor where, courteous sir, to find you," said Gawain. "I'll tell you when you've swung your stroke, and if you lift my large axe high and sever with one swing my tresses from my trunk, maybe I shall cease and you may rest here always." The green knight gayly got down, and tossed his lovely locks over his head, baring his powerful neck. Anchoring his left foot firmly on the ground, Gawain lifted the large axe high and brought it down. The sharp steel shattered the bones, sliced through the skin and severed the head from the trunk. The green head rolled about on the castle floor, while blood burst in spurts from the green man's neck. He neither flinched nor fell, but stood right up, steered straight to his head and siezed it in one hand. With his other hand he grabbed his bright green bridle, and, slipping his foot in a silver stirrup, mounted his strong green steed. He brandied his bulk about, head and body badly bleeding; as the courtiers felt great doubt, and his movements started reading.

Holding his head high in his hand, the green knight twisted it toward the royal table. He lifted his green eyelids and with a broad stare spoke of the sport the knights had made. "Gawain, you promised to pursue me in one year, pledged in truth before these knights to stand a stroke from me. Men call me Knight of the Green Chapel. Come with courage there to call on me or forever be called a miscreant." With a riotous rout, he reined and turned, rode through the large room's door, his head held high in his hand. The fire on the flint floor from his horse's hooves flashed even in the darkness as the green knight rode away. The King and Gawain then, laughed loud at the green knight's game; and all the other men, never saw life quite the same.

The year's first day passed and its last day was coming soon. First Christmas comes and then crabbed Lent, suffering the flesh with fish and plain, peeled herbs. Winter weather comes and clay grows hard with cold; and then clouds climb upwards and rain rushes down, falling on fields and folds in showers soft and warm. Flowers form on vines grown green, and birds sing sweetly busy building nests. The summer speeds on Zephyr winds, and creatures savor sunshine. Harvest hastes in quickly, high winds make war with clouds before the sun, leaves loose and light on ground no longer green. Then all that grew grows old when winter whirls this world we know. And so came Michelmas moon, with winter's chilly rage; reminding Gawain that soon, he must travel for his wage.

Yet, Gawain lingered with Arthur until All Hallow's Day, and he made fine fare on that high feast, with the revels and the riches of the great Round Table. After the mirth and the meal and the mourning of courteous knights and comely ladies sorry to see him leave, Gawain mentioned the voyage he had to make. "Liege, lord of my life, I ask now leave of you. You know the cost of this case: I am bound to bare my bones to our green guest, and give him back his game, as God doth wish." Then all the best of the castle bowed together, Awayne and Eric and many others. Lancelot and Lyonel and Lucan the Good lamented the leaving of gallant Gawain. These many bold men, the courageous company of the court, came forth together to give counsel to Gawain. Gawain said with good cheer, "Why should I hesitate? Our destiny's harsh, but dear, and I must embrace my fate."

Gawain dwelt there all day and dressed on the morn, asking early for his arms, all of which his servants brought with ceremony. First the servants spread a red silken carpet upon the floor, and much was the gold that glistened and shiny the steel placed on it. They brought his coat of mail, his burnished brass arm-pieces, his gray silk gloves embroidered with gold and a silver studded harness for his haughty horse Gringolet. Then Gawain spurred his steed and sprung on his way, so quickly the stones in the courtyard sparked. The other knights said, "By Christ, it is a shame that the noblest of men upon the earth, faultless in his five senses and fearing of the Lord, should seek out and suffer a savage stroke." He left without delay, following a twisted path; and I have heard men say, he feared no demon's wrath.

Now rode this noble knight through the land of Logres, Sir Gawain, in God's name, though it seemed no game to him. Often he found no food to fill his hunger, nor a soul to speak to as he sped on his way. The knight had no companions except his haughty horse and the fear of God, until he drew close to the wilderness of Wales. Then riding to the right of crags and copper cliffs, he rode across a river to the wilds of Wyral, where men of humble heart made homes. He asked kind knights, plain peasants and monied merchants he passed on his path, if they might in memory mark the grounds of the green chapel. Gawain traveled forests strange, where living creatures are never seen; but his goal refused to change, until he saw the chapel green.

He climbed many cliffs in strange countries, and on the bank of every river he found a foe so fierce and foul he had to fight. He warred with wolves that ran through the wilds, with bulls and boars that broke through bare-branched bushes, and with wild men of the woods who encountered him on crags. But winter was a worse wrath than those he warred with. Cold, clear water cascaded from the clouds, freezing as it fell to earth. The sleet half slayed him, knocked all night against his armor. Icicles fell on his face. He prayed aloud to God when the winter weather woke him.Then to Mary he made a moan, a knightly kind of prayer; to find him a friendly home, food, fire and folk who care.

Mounting merrily on the morn, he rode through a forest full and deep, wonderfully wild. High hills rose all about him, rough, ragged and covered with moss; and birds not blithe cried on brown, bare branches. He crossed himself three times hoping that Christ would grant him speed, carry him to a comfortable castle, so he could mend his soul at holy mass. Hardly had he crossed himself thrice when he descried, perched on a palisade with palings all around, the comliest castle a knight had ever seen, and the prettiest park, stretching two miles in all directions. The stronghold shimmered through sturdy sycamores, sweetgums and sasafras, and Gawain lifted his eyes in thanks to his savior. He called and soon there came, a porter pure and pleasant; who inquired quick of Gawain his name and where he hailed from.

"Good sir," Gawain responded, "I have journeyed long and wonder if your liege lord will let me lay one night in this fair castle." The drawbridge for Gawain was lowered, and Gawain and Gringolet entered the yard. On frozen ground good servants knelt to greet him, granting the good knight the graces he deserved. Gawain marked the man who made him welcome, a stern, stalwart knight with a broad, bright face and a beard as brown as beaver. Sheer silken cloths skillfully stitched with gold hung in the chamber where they showed Gawain. They lent him regal robes of priceless patterns to don for dinner with his host. They thought, "How he came here, required courage and might; and he seems without a peer, on fields where fierce men fight."

After mass and the merriest of meals, the lord of the castle asked Gawain whither he was wending, and what high adventure carried him so far from Arthur's courageous court. The host said he was honored that good Gawain rode Gringolet into the castle on Christ's own birthday. "By God's own grace," said Gawain, "to tell the truth, I seek a giant green, the Knight of the Green Chapel I must meet on New Year's day. In all the land of Logres, may the good Lord give me help, no fiercer foe has any seen. This man all green will suffer me a savage stroke, but I know not where to find him or his fold." The host said, "Until New Year's stay, for he dwells two miles from here; I'll show you the easy way, may the Lord all Christians fear."

Full glad then was Gawain, and graciously granted his host to be his guest for three days, and he thanked him truly for this above all things. He bowed and said his host's bidding was his bright and beautiful burden. His host held Gawain's hand hard and came up with a compact, a plan for each to present the other presents. But Gawain said he had no riches with him. Happily the host said, "I prefer the present of your truth, and ask you to agree to share the same with me. You rest here while I go hunting, and each night as it falls give unto me what you have won that day. I'll give the same to you." And as he fell asleep, the agreement filled his head; his promise good Gawain would keep, for in three days he might be dead.

Next morning before dawn the castle started awakening. Those sleeping there turned toward the darkness brightening in the window. Bercilac, lord of the castle, motioned his men into morning mass. Brief breakfasts followed mass and, as dawn's first light shone through sycamores beyond the castle, the host sat high on his haughty horse. Pleasant pages blew bugles as the kennels were unlocked; hounds barked and bayed in the castle courtyard. Wild beasts in the woods fled the barking and baying, bounding through thickets as fast arrows flew. The host forbad killing bucks with broad antlers, and, after the hunters' arrows all had flown, only doe were dead. The huntsmen with hatchets butchered the beasts, hacking at heads, as is the custom, and giving the foul flesh to the ravens. At the fork of the animals' thighs, they loosened the extra skin; and then with knives and eyes, sought the tender meat within.

Thus the lord through leafless forests enjoyed his sport, while Gawain lingered lazily, comfortable in a courtly, canopy bed. In his soft slumber he heard a scratch at his door, which opened shyly. He heaved his head out of the covers, and opened the bed curtain cautiously at its corner, waiting warily to see who might be sneaking in. It was the lord's lady, lovely to behold. She closed the door behind her, bowing towards the curtained bed. Courageous Gawain blushed crimson, sinking softly back beneath the covers, silent and still as someone asleep. The queen came quietly through the curtains, laid her full length down beside Gawain and watched him, waiting for him to waken. Our hero lay there long in pretended sleep, then made believe he was starting to stretch, and then feigned to be startled when he swiveled and suddenly saw her. Her chin and cheeks so sweet, were colored a maidenly red; and seemed strange laying down to greet, a stranger in her husband's bed.

"Good morning, Sir Gawain," said the queen quite gaily, "you sleep so soundly it was easy slipping secretly beside you. My husband and his hunters have gone chasing harts and does. My servants still slumber and the chamber door is locked. And since I'm secretly alone with the haughty knight that even elegant men honor, I should like to learn your loving ways. My body I offer thee, if you like your pleasure take; for your servant I shall be, and your appetite I shall slake."

"By my faith," said Gawain, "I am full flattered, but I think I am unworthy of this graciously offered gift — your fine, fair flesh. And besides, my fair one, you're married to a marvelous and kind man, a king more courteous than any knight." The lady spoke as though she loved him surely, and Gawain gave her witty and wise answers. They spoke at length of love and all things lovely, until the lady asked his leave, saying she would steal away secretly. But when she stood and started to leave the chamber, she turned around suddenly and stared at Gawain. "You're wonderful with words, handsome and well-mannered. But I know you can't be Sir Gawain." "Pray, tell why not," said the gallant knight, shocked by the lady's strange statement. The queen asked, "How could a man of manners, someone as gallant as Gawain, linger with a lady and not ask for a kiss. Such conduct would surely be considered rude." Gawain honorably agreed to a kiss, imagining the lady's need; must bring her king great bliss, and surely his hunger feed.

She slipped out quickly and Gawain called his chamberlain, who carried in his clothes. Gawain dressed quickly and bounded blithely off to mass, and then engaged in merry talk with ladies well born and bred. At moonrise the king and his men returned, their horses hooves sending sparks from the courtyard stones. Then the lord of the castle summoned all to stand beside him. The knights and ladies and maidens gathered round the courteous king. The king said, "Gawain, I give you the wild game I won today, my prizes from the forest — sweet venison and birds. Do you like the gift I give to you this night?"

"I've known no one to take such game in seven seasons of winter, and I accept your prize and commend you to the Lord," Gawain rejoined. And the king said sweetly, "Have you won any prizes to give to me today?" Gawain walked right up to the king, wrapped his arms around him and kissed him. "I give you the prize I won today," said Gawain, "and I hope you grant my gift is gracious." The king, the knights and the ladies all laughed, and much merriment was made while the sweet meats cooked. They sat by the chimney fire and sipped red wine, Gawain and the king, saying that on the morrow they would again give to each other the gracious gifts they won that day. The fire slowly burned, as the sturdy knights grew tired; and slipping into sleep they yearned, their hopes for the morrow fired.

Next morning, before the cry of the castle cock, the king and his huntsmen sat high on their horses. The hounds were let loose and leaped through the forest, finding at last a scent in a thicket of thorns. The huntsmen followed the hounds to a crag beneath a barren cliff, where a bold, wild boar braced himself for their attack. The archers fired arrows at the fearful beast. The hounds barked and bayed and the boar charged Bercilac, who killed the beast with his long lance. They charged through the forest seeking daring deeds, while Gawain slept sweetly in his royal chamber. The lady, looking lovely as ever, slipped into Gawain's curtained bed, and the knight felt he had never been by such temptation led. Gawain and the lady exchanged gay good mornings and spoke sweetly of passion and honor, and the queen, when she asked leave, gave Gawain a true tender kiss. When the lady left, Gawain quickly dressed and joyfully went to mass, and, as the huntsmen hurried through darkening, wild woods, our hero chatted gaily with comely ladies and their maids. At nightfall the lord returned amid laughter and merrily called for Gawain. He gave Gawain the gift of the brave, bold boar and asked for his present in return. Gawain kissed the king on the neck, saying, "Again I've kept our compact and gave you what I won today, a charming

Der vier beucker der do staels der hieß heintz
vnd was ein Salbuett

conquest." The king laughed heartily and the courtiers raised a merry toast as the wild pig turned on the spit above the fire. The lord said, "Gallant knight, you surely must be rich; you win kisses while I fight, giving gifts without a hitch."

During a merry meal and much mellow mead, Gawain asked to leave on the morrow, for it was New Year's Eve and a joyless journey had to be made. The lord convinced the knight his ride to the green chapel would be short, and told him he could wait until New Year's morning. All toasted this happy thought, as more mead made its way around the table. Gawain went to bed and slept soft and sound, and the lord rose early, anxious for the hunt. After mass the huntsmen mounted and unleashed the hounds, who followed the footprints of a wily fox. They chased the fox all day, riding with daring over rocks and ragged ravines. The lord finally killed the miserable animal, which the hounds fell upon, leaving only the hide. At the castle, Gawain lay resting, sweet reveries filling his head; but he was due for a testing, and the green knight caused him dread.

At dawn the queen, more lovely than ever, came into his room, slipping sweetly into his curtained bed. Gems glowed in her fair hair and her shoulders and breasts were beautiful and bare. Gawain made efforts to console the comely queen, who had come to offer her love once more. "May my strength resist her charms," Gawain silently prayed. After pleasant talk, the lady perceived that gallant Gawain didn't care for her curves and charms, rare though she knew they were. Before she left his bed, she kissed the knight sweetly, saying, "If you don't want to love me, for my sake love yourself. Take my magic girdle: no harm can come to any man that wears it." When she was gone, Gawain dressed quickly, hiding the magic girdle under his tunic, and confessed and heard mass. The huntsmen returned with fine fun and fanfare, and the lord called Gawain and gave him the fox's hide. All toasted the gift merrily and waited to see gallant Gawain's next gift. Again the good Gawain kissed the king and hugged him hard, saying "Lord, we are even, and now I leave to meet the green knight, who shan't hurt me if heaven is watching." But the lord told him to wait till morning, and Gawain agreed, sinking into sound sleep after good food and tall talk. The good knight woke at dawn. Thanking the lord and saying farewell, a servant as his guide; and imagining the jaws of hell, to the Green Chapel he began his ride.

Dawn's darkness and wild winds whipped through the woods; dreary was the weather that New Year's Day. The cold was keen and the clay beneath haughty Gringolet's hooves was hard. Clad in his arms, Gawain followed the servant through sweetgums and sassafras, straight sycamores and old, gnarled oaks. Mists moved among the moors, and suddenly the servant, great fear in his green eyes, spoke swiftly to Gawain: "Brave knight, a demon dwells in that Green Chapel, a foe so fierce I'll go no further with you. Why don't you flee? I'll never tell a living man, and surely your soul will not be soiled for avoiding that green friend of Satan." The servant pointed the way, toward a hill beside a stream; and once alone the knight did pray, half thinking the place a dream.

He moved along the swift stream and made out a mound, and there he reined his horse and rode through lindens brown and bare, until he reached the strange rise in the frozen, wide ravine. Gawain thought the devil himself resided in the spot, and cursed the foul mound as the devil's cruel church. The massive mound rose steeply beside the stream, and two huge holes led into the uncivilized structure. Gawain felt the fiend with his five senses, fearing the cursed chapel that had been his quest. The stream bubbled as though it were boiling, and over a wall of rocks water fell fast and furious, thundering and foaming in the boiling brook. Driven to keep his awful appointment, Gawain drew back his reins and dutifully dismounted, debating his delivery to the sorrowful spot he saw. "Good Lord," said the gentle knight, "this mound has an hellish air; no doubt the devil might, where I stand raise his demon prayer."

"Damned desolate indeed," Gawain thought in silence. "This spot fits the fiend and his foul friends." He rose on foot to the roof of that weed-rankled residence, recoiling when he heard raucous noises resounding from a rock beyond the foaming brook. Like someone sharpening a sword or a scythe on stone, the grinding sound whirred wildly in the woods, shattering the silence and strengthening Gawain's soul. It was a whirring noise, like water rushing through a mill, or a burnished blade on a whetstone. "By God," said Gawain, "this grinding goes on for me. I wonder when this whirring wail will end, and who waits here for me. For God's sake," said Gawain, "the devil must be here; but here I shall remain, for I have no time to fear."

Then Gawain courageously called out: "Who rules this wretched and malicious mound? Make speed if you seek something from me, and feel full sure I'll not linger here." "Be patient virtuous knight," said a voice he couldn't see, "vouchsafe me silence until I sharpen my steel for the stroke you owe me." The whir of the whetting stone went on for a while, and when the weapon's sharpness suited him, the green knight came quickly, crossing a crag above a cedar-shaded crevice. The green knight stalked through the swirling stream, fording it fast to face Sir Gawain. The knight, as before, was all green — his garments, his face and his fierce figure. Long green locks fell over his sturdy shoulders; his stern eyes stared as they had from his severed head. With a ferocious face and his weapon, the green knight made haste across a stretch of snow and cedar to greet Gawain, who cringed with each crunch of the green knight's footfalls. Sir Gawain and the green knight met, but our hero didn't bow; then the green knight quickly said, "I get the truth of your spirit now."

"Gawain," said the green knight, "may the good Lord guide you, you truly timed your travel to this place, and there are no seconds by this stream to spoil the sport between us. Recall our arrangement — I'm sure you remember it, gallant Gawain — and how on New Year's Day you said you would suffer me a stroke with an axe at your head. Hold your helmet in your hand, good Gawain. Go down on your knees."

"By God," said Gawain, "get on with your gory game, and I shall stand you a single stroke, strike once but strike no more, or I shall stroke at you." Gawain then lowered his head, before the gruesome green knight; determined to hide his dread, with courage if he might.

Steadying himself, the green man swiftly swung the axe, which hovered high over his haughty head. Gawain glanced sideways at the shadow of its shaft and his shoulders shrank from the savage stroke. The green knight checked his swing, saying, "You can't be Gawain, the gay and gallant and gracious knight, that noble soul who never shrinks no matter what the strife. I can't believe such cowardice could overcome that knight. I didn't shrink from your strong stroke, even though it severed my head." Gawain said, "I flinched once, but I will flinch no more; though I cannot match your stunts, and my own severed head restore."

"Get on with your grisly game, green knight, and give good your stroke. Deal me my destiny without delay. Swing your strongest stroke and I shall not shrink from it. Fiercely the green knight raised his great axe, and as fiercely forced it down, stopping his swing before it scratched Gawain's skin. Gawain gave all his strength to standing the stroke. Stone-still, he saw the shadow stop above his skin. "You didn't shudder just now," the green knight said, "so I think you ready now to lose your head, as I in Arthur's court lost mine."

"Get on with it, green man," Gawain shouted in anger. "Save your silly speech and swing your sharpened steel." The green knight lifted the weapon lightly, letting it down swiftly on Gawain's smooth skin, slicing it only slightly. Gawain stood still as blood seeped across his shoulders. He saw his blood spot the pure white snow beneath him. Then he leapt the length of a lance and drew his sword, saying to the green knight, "You've swung your stroke, the next one I'll return. Green man, you've had your swing, one for one as we agreed; try another and harm you'll bring, like mine, your neck will bleed."

The green knight leaned on his hatchet's handle, steadying himself on his steel axe's shaft. He looked longingly at Gawain, bold and brave though bedeviled, and the sight did the green man's heart great good. "Bold baron, you needn't be so fierce on this field," the green knight said, "no man here has treated you maliciously. I've kept the compact we made in Arthur's court, and, caring about honor, you came here courageously. I release you from your obligation, though I could have hacked your head off with a harsher blow had I a heavy heart and hand. My first feint with this steel stems from the deal we made that first night: you kept your compact and kissed me. My second stroke stems from the second night, when you kissed me in good faith, fully keeping your worthy word and giving the gift you won from my wife. Twice I only pretended to swing, for two nights you honored our deal; but my third stroke gave you a sting, for the girdle you tried to steal."

"That girdle that guards you belongs to me: my worthy wife wove it. And I know well your wooing, for I sent my wife to tempt you with the wiley ways of women. I think, Gawain, you're as faultless as any knight I know. Twice you lay long with my lovely wife and came away untainted. You lowered yourself only to lascivious conduct, taking the girdle as your guard, for love of your own life. For that no man can blame you." Gawain gazed in amazement at the green knight as he spoke, and, ashamed, he blushed full crimson. "I confess that cowardice conquered all my virtue, and I curse the fears that found me full untrue," said Gawain. He untied the green girdle and threw it to the knight. "I confess to you green knight, my cowardice and lies; actions of my soul's foul fright, before the Good Lord's eyes."

The green knight sweetly smiled, looking softly upon Gawain. "I consider you clean and completely purified, Gawain. You've confessed your faults with much more care than any. I give you now my green girdle, woven with gold along its edges. Take it as a token of the true trust that passed between the two of us today."

"May God repay you for your gift," Gawain replied. "The sin it signifies, shall stay forever in my sight: the frailty of the flesh, the fear of deeds done right."

The green knight told Gawain that Morgana Le Fay, who slept with the wizard Merlin and stole his powers, engineered this great enchantment, wanting to test the truth of Arthur's knights. And then he invited Gawain back to his castle, where they could make much merriment. But Gawain had lingered too long, and asked leave to go his way; the two knights stern and strong, vowed for each other to pray.

Through the world's wild winds and wicked ways, Gawain and Gringolet hurried home. Many adventures befell them, but I shall not tell them now. Excitement spread through Arthur's court when gallant Gawain rode into the castle's courtyard. The King and Queen both kissed their courageous kin, and all the knights and ladies gathered around. Gawain gave them all the gory tale, explained the lovely lady who lay each day beside him, and the secret girdle that he stole: the sign of his sin and shame. The knights and ladies laughed, for worthier than any was the weakness of Gawain. All the knights then promised that from that day on, they would go forth with a green girdle, a garment to recall Sir Gawain's great courage. Many adventures like this one, have fallen from a kiss; may He above us and His Son, bring all men holy bliss. AMEN.

# Parsival at the Castle of the Grail

*Destined to become the protector of the Grail, Parsival chanced on the holy relic before he was mature enough to become its guardian. This depiction of Parsival's encounter with the Grail is from Wolfram von Eschenbach's* Parsival.

hoever cares to listen to where Lady Fortuna is leading Parsival now will hear of wonders and marvels. Let the son of Gahmuret ride on. Large-hearted people will wish him great luck, for he will suffer before he achieves honor and joy. One thought only troubled him: that already he was so far from a woman more beautiful and virtuous than any other, alive or written of in books. Thoughts of the queen strained his wits, which he would have lost completely if he weren't so courageous. The horse dragged his reins over swamps and fallen trees, for his rider's hands did nothing to guide him. According to the legend, Parsival rode farther that day than a bird could have flown.

Would you like to hear what is happening to him now? At dusk he came to a lake. Fishermen who owned the lake were anchored in its middle. By the time they noticed him at the edge of the lake, he was close enough for them to hear whatever he said. One of the fishermen wore clothes so splendid that even if he were king of all who lived they couldn't have been more magnificent. Peacock feathers adorned his hat. Parsival addressed himself to the beautifully dressed fisherman, asking him to direct him, in the name of God and friendliness, to where he could find shelter for the night.

The fisherman, who seemed more sorrowful than any man, answered Parsival quickly: "Sir, I know of no human dwellings within thirty miles of here, but there's an old stone castle nearby. You have no place to go but there, and besides, where else could you go before nightfall? Follow this wall of rock to its end, then pull the right rein of your horse. When you reach the moat, where I imagine you will have to halt, ask the attendant to lower the drawbridge, then follow the road."

Thanking the fisherman for his advice, he turned his horse toward the wall of stone, hearing the fisherman say: "If you get to the castle I'll act as your host, and you can thank me after your stay if you then feel I treated you well. Be careful as you ride: the paths around here lead nowhere, and the cliff beside you is very steep. I would be sorry to see anything happen to you." Parsival spurred his horse to a brisk trot, followed the fisherman's directions and arrived at the moat, where he saw the raised drawbridge.

With walls so smooth they looked as though turned on a lathe, the castle was the most impregnable fortification Parsival had ever seen. Nothing could succeed in attacking it, except perhaps a bird or a flying instrument of war. Fortified turrets and enclosures appeared everywhere along the castle, and it seemed to Parsival that if all the world's armies laid siege to it those inside could hold out against attack for thirty years.

A squire approached Parsival and asked him what he wanted and where he came from. "The fisherman told me to come here," Parsival replied, "and he told me that when I arrived the drawbridge would be lowered and I could ride in and lodge for the night."

"Sir, if the fisherman sent you have no fear that you will be welcomed here, and honored. For the sake of the fisherman we will attend to your every need, your every comfort." The squire lowered the drawbridge.

Parsival rode across the drawbridge and into the castle's courtyard, which was large and covered with trimmed green grass, untrammeled by the horse hooves of knightly sports. Jousts never took place on this grass, nor did knightly pennants blow in the wind. The courtyard hadn't seen a knightly tournament for many years, because the knights who lived there were stricken with grief. The castle's inhabitants, however, did nothing to make Parsival share in their grief. Rather, knights both old and young greeted him warmly and rushed to be the first to take his horse's reins. Several knights led Parsival to a chamber, where they skilfully removed his armor. When his armor was removed, the knights marveled at Parsival's youth, his beardless beauty, and agreed he was blessed.

The young man asked his attendants for water, and then washed his armor's rust from his face and hands. When Parsival finished washing, his attendants looked at him in amazement, believing that from him a beautiful new day was dawning, so handsome and exemplary was his beauty. They gave him a priceless tunic of Arabian silk, which the youth drew about him. He left the tie-cords hanging loose, and for that the attendants praised him.

The attendants poured Parsival drink, asked after his every need, and explained the tunic belonged to the queen, who would have ordered an even more priceless garment made for Parsival had she known in advance he was due to arrive and bless the castle. They removed his armor, which Parsival regretted moments later when one of the attendants made a joke that Parsival took to be an insult. Not finding his sword at hand, Parsival clenched his fist so furiously that blood gushed from his fingernails, and just in time to save his fellow squire from a beating someone explained to Parsival:

"Fair sir," said the squire, "do not take anger at that remark. This fellow likes to joke and make merry, even though the rest of us have heavy hearts. He was merely trying to tell you the fisherman has arrived. You are the fisherman's honored guest. Forget about your anger and go take your ease beside him."

They followed stairs up to a great hall that was lit by a hundred chandeliers, which illuminated from above the fisherman's household. Small candles were burning all along the walls. Parsival saw a hundred couches spread throughout the room, each covered with a lovely quilt, capable of sitting four knights and surrounded by a round carpet. No expense had been spared in decorating the room, which had three fireplaces made of marble, each aglow with large glowing logs of cedar. Parsival had never seen such beautiful fires. The fisherman entered the hall and was seated by attentive squires on a couch facing the central fireplace. His happiness no longer existed, for the fisherman was more dead than alive.

"Come sit here beside me," said the sorrowful host, "for I would be treating you as a stranger if I asked you to place yourself farther away than right here beside me."

Because of his ailment, the fisherman kept huge fires burning always, and he wrapped himself in clothes lined inside and out with sable and mink skins. The least extravagant of his furs, black and gray otter, would fetch high prices in any market. The fisherman's hat was also trimmed with expensive furs, as well as Arabian brocade adorned with rubies.

The opulent hall, filled with splendid knights, suddenly became the scene of a sorrowful spectacle. Through one of the hall's doors a page rushed in bearing a lance, which pierced with sorrow the happiness of all present. Blood poured from the point of the lance, flowed down its shaft and seeped into the fabric of the page's sleeve. Weeping and wailing filled the large hall: the people of thirty lands could not have shed so many tears. Bearing the lance high in his hands the page walked around the entire perimeter of the large hall, leaving, finally, when he reached the door he had entered through. The mournful moans of those in the room ceased when the lance, which reminded them of the reasons for their sorrow, was no longer in the hall.

If the tale won't weary you, I will describe with what great ceremony the fisherman's court was served. At the far end of the great hall a steel door opened, and two maidens entered, each of noble birth and so beautiful I could never hope to describe them. Their hair was decorated with nothing but flowers, and each carried a golden candelabra, whose candle's flames bent backward as they walked. Wavy, long and beautiful, their hair fell down around their shoulders, but let me not forget to describe the clothes they wore. The countess of Tenebroc and the woman who walked beside her were dressed in brown woolen gowns, tied tight around the waist with a girdle. Following these long-haired ladies, was a duchess and her companion, each of whom had lips red as fire, carrying in their hands ivory stools. With heads bent, the four ladies placed their trestles before the fisherman royally, attending to every wish. Then they stood together in a group, each dressed in the same way, each beautiful.

But look, four more pairs of ladies entered the great hall. Four of the ladies carried a huge candelabra, the other four carried among them a precious stone so clear it seemed the very light of day shone through it. It was a garnet-hyacinth, cut so thinly it could serve as a table top. This is the table at which the fisherman ate. The ladies placed the garnet-hyacinth tabletop on the ivory trestles and then stepped back, bowing to the fisherman. Each of the ladies wore flowers in their hair, and generously-cut robes of green samite tied about the waist with jeweled girdles.

The daughters of two counts approached the fisherman. Each was beautiful beyond description, and they carried, on linen napkins, knives fashioned of white silver, each of them sharpened so well they could have cut right through steel. Four other lovely maidens carried a light for the silver settings, and all six maidens waited before the fisherman, anxious to tend to his needs. The maidens all bowed, and the two who held the silver knives laid them down on the gem-carved table. All the maidens, sixteen of them if I counted right, then withdrew, but look: six more are entering the hall, dressed in silk from the Holy Land woven generously with gold.

Then the queen entered, radiant, glowing as brilliantly as the dawn, clothed in a flowing robe of Arabian silk. On a golden plate covered with deep green silk she carried the perfection of Paradise, the Holy Grail, the most wonderful of earthly things. This was the nature of the Holy Grail: that she who watched over it had to be utterly pure and above all manner of falsity.

Lights entered the hall before the Grail, six clear glass vials with balsam burning within them, shedding a beautiful light. The queen with the Holy Grail and the maidens carrying the balsam lights bowed gracefully, and then the queen placed the Grail before the fisherman. The legend has it that Parsival couldn't take his eyes off the lady, the queen who carried the Grail, although he thought to himself he did so because he was wearing one of her garments. The maidens arranged themselves in a semicircle around the queen, inclined their sinuous necks more elegantly than I could tell, and withdrew.

Each group of four knights assembled in the hall was attended to by a squire bearing a golden basin, and beside each squire there was a well-groomed page holding white linen napkins. Other squires carried into the room a hundred tables, and the pages spread white linens upon them. The host, who had long since given up all hopes of joy, washed his hands and Parsival, in the same water washed his. A squire knelt immediately before them, offering them a bright, colored silk towel, which a noble king had given the fisherman as a gift. In the spaces between the many tables, squires stood ready to serve those sitting. Four squires stood waiting — two knelt and carved, two brought drink and other victuals.

Four carts were wheeled into the great hall, each one weighed down with drinking cups of gold. And then a hundred squires in turn passed before the Grail: each of them held a white linen napkin, and each was granted by the Grail a loaf of bread. I will tell you exactly as I was told: whoever reached out before the Grail found in his hand exactly what he wished for, warm food or cold, venison or duck, tender or gamey meats. "Such a thing is impossible you might say," but you are wrong, for the Holy Grail is the very cup of Paradise, a horn of such abundance and such delights as only those in heaven have seen.

Gravies, delicate sauces and fruits appeared in golden vessels. Whoever held his cup before the Grail found it full seconds later with the drink of his desire, whether mead, transparent wine or the juice of the mulberry. Large appetites and small were satisfied to perfection, for those in the fisherman's hall were served by the power of the Grail.

Parsival took in the wonders of the Grail but, in the name of good breeding and tasteful conduct, refrained from asking any questions. Parsival thought to himself how his previous host, with whom he had stayed four months, had warned him not to ask too many questions. He thought that if he stayed with the fisherman for a long time he would learn things without having to ask questions. In the middle of his private thoughts, Parsival noticed a squire approaching him. The squire was carrying a sword whose sheath was carved of a single ruby and whose hilt was wondrous. The fisherman took the sword from the squire and presented it to Parsival, saying:

"Sir, before God wounded me I wielded this sword in the heat of battle, You deserve it, and once you feel its balance you will never want to be without it in this world where men do battle."

Even as he grasped the sword and wondered at it, Parsival didn't ask the question. Receiving the sword was a sign for Parsival to ask, and one has to pity not only Parsival but also the fisherman, who would have been freed from his pain had Parsival asked him the question.

The feast was ending. Servants appeared and rearranged the hundred couches, and collected the golden goblets; and the beautiful maidens appeared, and took away the dishes on the four carts. As they had before, the maidens led the queen to the Grail, then bowed before the fisherman and Parsival. Parsival watched the maidens and the queen exit through the door they had entered by and, before a squire closed the door behind them, Parsival saw in the room they entered the most beautiful old man he had ever seen. The old man's hair was white as snow; he was reclining on a couch.

The feast was ending on as sorrowful a note as it had begun: everyone seemed sad beyond redemption. The fisherman looked mournfully upon Parsival, saying, "Your bed is ready for you, and if you feel tired I suggest that you sleep." It was a great pity that they parted like this, a tragic event that augured ill for them both.

Parsival bowed before his host, thanked him for his gifts and courtesy, and followed several knights to his room, which was rich and sumptuous beyond description. The silken bedspread glowed like fire. Parsival wished the knights who escorted him to his room a good night, and then allowed the pages to undress him gently. They wondered at Parsival's fairness of hair and complexion. Not even the candles outshone the radiant young knight. After the pages left the room, four maidens, each preceded by a squire, entered. Each of the maidens carried a candle, but when Parsival saw the four women he leapt under the bed covers, until the maidens said: "Please stay awake for a little while." Parsival pulled the covers from over his head and his bright, handsome face made all the maidens sigh. The redness of his mouth and the smoothness of his skin captured the maidens' hearts, and they wondered at how young the noble knight was. There wasn't a single whisker on his face.

In their white hands the maidens handed to Parsival delicate wines, sweet juices and, wrapped in a white silk cloth, fruits that only grow in Paradise. Parsival asked one of the maidens to sit down, but she responded that it were best that she didn't. All the maidens stood about watching the knight as he drank of the wines and the juices, and nibbled on a fruit. After a time the maidens withdrew; the pages also left, leaving behind two burning candles at the foot of Parsival's bed.

But Parsival didn't sleep alone: deep distress lay like a weight on his body until dawn. The suffering that would soon beleaguer Parsival appeared in his sleep as nightmares. He dreamt of swords piercing his armor, of lances shattering his shield, of pains worse than death. Misery lay beside him through the night. These terrible dreams finally awoke him; sweat had soaked the silken sheets; daylight was in the windows. Parsival wondered where the pages were. "Who will bring me my clothes," he called aloud, "who will strap on my rusty armor?" Parsival fell back to sleep for a short time, awoke again and called out for the pages. There was nobody around. Parsival stood up from bed and saw on the vermillon Persian rug his armor, his clothes and two swords, his own and the one the fisherman had given him.

"Why have they left me alone in this room, with no one to help me on with my armor? I suffered in my sleep so terribly that there surely must be great evil awaiting me this day. If enemies are besieging the fisherman, I would certainly do battle for his cause." He spoke aloud like this for some minutes, then quickly armed himself from head to foot, certain that trouble and battles were about to take place. He strapped on both swords. At the foot of the stairs outside his room, his horse was tethered; his lance and shield leaned against the near wall. Parsival, before mounting his horse, ran through the castle yelling for someone to tell him where everybody was. No one answered. Parsival was angry, although he knew not why, when he discovered the castle was empty, and when he rode out the gate the grass that had been untrampled by horses the day before had been ridden over by hundreds of hooves. Parsival was screaming with anger, and rode his horse hard toward the drawbirdge, which suddenly crashed open as he approached it. The bridge was drawn up again the instant Parsival's horse cleared it, and the knight reined his horse in and turned around to see why someone had almost flung him and his horse into the moat. He was so angry he drew his sword.

"Keep riding," said a squire who had been hidden among the ropes that worked the drawbridge, "and know that you bear the hatred of the sun. You are a simpleton. Why didn't you ask the fisherman the question? Obviously you didn't want to win great honor."

Parsival shouted back at the squire, demanding an explanation, but the squire disappeared without answering. Parsival shouted to him again, and then again, but the only sound that came back was the squire's vanishing footfalls. "An unfortunate parting," Parsival thought, but it was more so than he realized, for he had lost much and will have to suffer a great deal before recapturing what he had. A throw of the dice had brought him to the Grail, but now like snake eyes Fortuna scowled on Parsival.

Parsival rode off, following closely the hoofprints on the trail, thinking, "The riders I'm following must be battling nobly for the fisherman's cause. Could they think their ranks would be weakened by my presence? I would battle with them to my very death, and earn the noble welcome they gave me and this miraculous sword, which as yet I haven't earned."

So Parsival, the purest of spirits, followed the hoofprints and his adventures began. Almost as soon as he started following them, the hoofprints grew fainter, barely visible, for the riders had apparently separated and gone off in different directions. The tracks of the riders became narrower and narrower, then disappeared. Then, out of nowhere, Parsival heard the voice of a woman crying. The leaves and grass were still wet with dew, and at the base of a linden tree the knight saw a maiden suffering great pain, the pain of love. She was holding in her arms a dead, embalmed knight. No one could have looked at her sitting there without feeling pity. Parsival pulled his left rein tight and turned toward the maiden, whom he didn't recognize even though he should have: she was his mother's sister's child. He brought his horse to a stop a few feet from the maiden, who didn't even acknowledge his presence until he spoke — so great was her grief.

"Lady, the sight of your grief and sorrow rends my heart in two. If there is any service I can offer you, command me as you will."

Tears welling from her eyelids, the maiden looked up. She thanked Parsival for his offer; asked what kingdom he had come from. "Traveling in this fierce wasteland is foolish, kind knight, for countless are the strangers who have died here, countless the powers that slayed them. Turn back toward where you came from if you value your life. Where did you spend the night?"

"In a castle not a mile from here," replied Parsival, "the richest and most fortified castle I've ever seen. I left there scarcely an hour ago "

"You shouldn't make fun, especially by lying, of one who has trusted you," said the lady to the knight. "Your shield is that of a foreigner, and if you hail from a civilized place this wasteland might easily have been too much for you. No trees were ever cut nor any stones hewn for thirty miles in any direction from here. No structure stands within this wasteland, except for one, which is rich in all manner of earthly perfections. No matter how diligently one seeks for it one will never find it, though many have tried. One can only chance upon it unawares, and you, fair knight, pretend never to have heard of it. Munsalvesche is the name of the castle. It was bequeathed by the aged Titurel to his son, a warrior who won great fame but died, finally, in a joust over love. He had four children, three of whom live in sorrow, the fourth in constant prayer. Trevizent is the name of the one who chose the path of monk and his brother, Anfortas, can't even ride or lay down — so thoroughly has he suffered God's will. If you indeed visited his castle, Anfortas, the fisherman, would have been freed of his terrible suffering."

Not knowing what to say, Parsival replied, "I saw in that castle more beautiful women than I ever thought existed, and miracles beyond compare. The fisherman gave me this sword."

The maiden finally recognized her cousin's voice. "Parsival? Tell me the truth, did you really see the Grail and the fisherman, he who has suffered more than any? Tell me the good news, for if his pain is ended you are blessed above all men. All kingdoms will be subject to your rule, and whatever moves through air — creatures tame and wild — will wait for your command. You will be beyond rich."

"Cousin, how ever did you recognize me?" Parsival said.

"I am the maiden who told you your name, who against your mother's wishes told you you were born to be a knight. When your father, the noblest knight of all, died in combat your mother made all her kin promise to tell you you were of common stock. Now look what God has done to me: my lover lays dead in my arms."

"Are you Sigune, who told me who I was? Why is your mouth no longer red, your hair no longer long and wavy? You have lost your loveliness and your color, but if I were holding a dead lover in my lap I'm sure I'd lose my character too. Sigune, your knight is dead—let us bury him." When Parsival finished speaking more tears flowed forth from Sigune's eyes. She hadn't even thought of burying her lover, and she stared at Parsival as though his offer to help her was madness. The knight didn't know what to say, but he didn't have to, for the lady spoke:

"If you want to bring me joy, Parsival, tell me that that sorrowful fisherman is free of his pain, that you have delivered that mournful man. You are wearing his sword, which you know has magical powers — powers that eliminate fear in battle. It's edges are perfectly parallel to each other. That sword was made by Trebuchet, the famous smith, and should it ever break, which it will if he who holds it is impure, it can be restored by holding it in the source of the river Lac. Do pennance first, and then hold the sword in the headwaters before the light of dawn has fallen on them. The sword has magical charms, but its user must know its secrets, which are the secrets of life. Tell me, Parsival, and don't be shy to reveal the great honor that is yours, of the miracles you saw and those you will in your lifetime do. You will want for nothing, neither riches nor royalty nor renown. No person on earth can compare to your achievement if you asked the question, as you should have."

Parsival said, "I didn't ask." He saw horror and pity in Sigune's eyes, and felt an emptiness in his soul.

forlui plaist il durement Et lore respondit une
dame alakorne et dist Dame pour dieu dont il
estre si bon chlr come vous dites. oul set lekoyne
Car il est detoutes pars extraiz du plus bon
dit du monde et du plus hault lignage que on
sache Et tant descendirent les dames et aleret
our bespres pour lahaultesse du iour Et
 quant le roy fut issu du monstier et il vint
au palais en hault si comanda qles nappes
fussent mises Et lors sallerent seoir les com
paignons chu en son lieu ainsi come il auo
ient fait au matin Et quant ilz se furent tot
assiz. lors oyrent vng estoir detonnaire si
grant et si merueilleux quil leur fu aduis q

le palais deust fondre Et maintenant entre ceulx
vng ray desouleil plus cler atent doubles quil
nyauoit deuant Si furent tantost par seins
aussi come sils fussent enluminez par lagce
du saint esprit Et comencerent a regarder
lun lautre Car ilz ne sauoient dont telle clarte
leur estoit venue Et ny ot celluy qui peust par
ler ne dire mot tant furent muetz comme et
retes Et quat demonues furet grat piece en
telle maniere que nul deulx nauoit pouoir de
parler ains regardoient tot come bestes mues

Comt le saint graal saparut aux chlrs de la
table ronde couuert dun blac samyt z ...
... entra leans le sang graal
... couuert dun blanc samit Mais
Il ny eust onques cellui qui
peust veoir qui la portoit Si y
entra par vng leguit huys du palais

eust cellui qui peut apperceuoir q le portoit z le
partir de toutes viandes ilz seoient demander
Et maintenant quil fust entres
fust le palais rempli desi bonnes
odeurs que se toutes les espices
du monde y feussent entrees et
espandues Et il ala tout entour

A ceste partye
nous dist lhis
toire que apres
ce que la nuit
du tournoiement
fu passee et que ce vint a len
demain matin le roy artus se
leua chaussa et vesty et lors quil

fu appareillie il oy la messe pre
mier œuure car il en estoit
coustumier Et pour ce le teno
ent tous ceulx qui le congnois
soient a moult preudomme tan
tost que la messe fu ditte et que
tous ses barons furet assemble
ou en partye il leur commenca

# The Death of Arthur

*The treachery of Sir Mordred and the last days of the Round Table are the subject of this excerpt from Sir Thomas Malory's* Morte D'Arthur.

ow Sir Mordred presumed and took on him to be king of England, and would have married the queen, his uncle's wife.

As Sir Mordred, during King Arthur's absence, was ruler of all England, he falsified letters, claiming they came from beyond the sea, letters that specified King Arthur was slain in battle with Sir Launcelot. Wherefore Sir Mordred made a parliament, and called the lords together, and there he made them to choose him king; and so was he crowned at Canterbury, and held a feast there fifteen days; and afterward he drew him unto Winchester, and there he took the queen, Guenever, and said plainly that he would wed her, his uncle's wife and his father's wife. And so he made ready for the feast, and a day prefixed that they should be wedded; wherefore Queen Guenever was passing heavy. But she durst not discover her heart, but spake fair, and agreed to Sir Mordred's will. Then she desired of Sir Mordred for to go to London, to buy all manner of things that longed unto the wedding. And by cause of her fair speech Sir Mordred trusted her well enough, and gave her leave to go. And so when she came to London she took the Tower of London, and suddenly in all haste possible she stuffed it with all manner of victual, and well garnished it with men, and so kept it. Then when Sir Mordred wist and understood how he was beguiled, he was passing wroth out of measure. And a short tale for to make, he went and laid a mighty siege about the Tower of London, and made many great assaults thereat, and threw many great engines unto them, and shot great guns. But all might not prevail for Sir Mordred, for Queen Guenever would never, for fair speech nor for foul, trust to come in his hands again. Then came the Bishop of Canterbury, the which was a noble clerk and a holy man, and thus he said to Sir Mordred: "Sir, what will ye do? Will ye first displease God and then shame yourself, and all knighthood? Is not King Arthur your uncle, no farther but your mother's brother, and on her himself King Arthur begat you, upon his own sister. Therefore how may you wed your father's wife?

"Sir," said the noble clerk, "leave this opinion or I shall curse you with book and bell and candle."

"Do thou thy worst," said Sir Mordred, "wit thou well I shall defy thee."

"Sir," said the Bishop, "and wit you well I shall not fear me to do that which I should. Also where ye noise where my lord Arthur is slain, and that is not so, and therefore ye will make a foul work in this land."

"Peace, thou false priest," said Sir Mordred, "chafe me any more and I shall strike off thy head."

So the Bishop departed and did the cursing in the proudest wise that might be done. And then Sir Mordred sought the Bishop of Canterbury, for to have him slain. Then the Bishop fled, and took part of his goods with him and went nigh unto Glastonbury; and there he was as priest hermit in a chapel, and lived in poverty and in holy prayers, for well he understood that mischievous war was at hand. Then Sir Mordred sought on Queen Guenever by letters and messages, and by fair means and foul means, for to have her to come out of the Tower of London; but all this availed not, for she answered him shortly, openly and privily, that she would rather slay herself than to be married with him.

Then came word to Sir Mordred that King Arthur had raised the siege against Sir Launcelot, and he was coming homeward with a great host, to be avenged upon Sir Mordred; wherefore Sir Mordred had his scribes write writs to all the barony of this land, and much people drew to him. For then was the common voice among them that with Arthur there was no other life but war and strife, and with Sir Mordred was great joy and bliss. Thus was Sir Arthur depraved, and evil said of. And many there were that King Arthur had made up of nought, and given them lands, who didn't then say a good word of him. Lo, ye all Englishmen, see ye not what a mischief here was! For he that was the most king and knight of the world, and most loved the fellowship of noble knights, and by him they were all upholden, now might not these Englishmen hold them content with him. Lo, thus was the old custom and usage of this land; and also men say that we of this land have not yet lost nor forgotten that custom and usage. Alas, this is a great default of us Englishmen, for there may be no thing that please us the full term. And so fared the people at that time— they were better pleased with Sir Mordred than they were with King Arthur; and much people drew unto Sir Mordred, and said they would abide with him for better and for worse. And so Sir Mordred drew with a great host to Dover, for there he heard say that Sir Arthur would arrive, and so he thought to beat his own father from his lands; and the most part of all England held with Sir Mordred, the people were so new fangle.

How after King Arthur had tidings, he returned and came to Dover, where Sir Mordred met him to attack his landing party; and of the death of Sir Gawaine.

And so as Sir Mordred was at Dover with his host, there came King Arthur with a great navy of ships, and galleys, and smaller ships. And there was Sir Mordred ready, waiting upon his landing, to let his own father to land upon the land that he was king over. Then there was launching of great boats and small, and full of noble men of arms; and there was much slaughter of gentle knights, and many a full bold baron was laid full low, on both parties. But King Arthur was so courageous that no manner of knights could keep him from landing, and his knights fiercely followed him; and so they landed despite Sir Mordred and all his power, and put Sir Mordred aback, so that he and all his people fled. So when this battle was done, King Arthur let bury his people that were dead. And then was noble Sir Gawaine found in a great boat, lying more than half dead. When Sir Arthur realized that Sir Gawaine was laid so low, he went unto him; and there the king made sorrow out of measure, and took Sir Gawaine in his arms, and thrice he there swooned.

And then when he awaked, he said: "Alas, Sir Gawaine, my sister's son, here now thou liest, the man in the world that I loved most; and now is my joy gone; for now, my nephew Sir Gawaine, I will discover me unto your person: in Sir Launcelot and you I most had my joy, and mine affiance, and now have I lost my joy of you both; wherefore all mine earthly joy is gone from me."

"Mine uncle King Arthur," said Sir Gawaine, "wit you well my death day is come, and all is through mine own hastiness and willfulness; for I am smitten upon the old wound that Sir Launcelot gave me, on which I feel sure I must die; and had Sir Launcelot been with you as he was, this unhappy war had never begun; and of all this am I the cause, for Sir Launcelot and his blood, through their prowess, held all your cankered enemies in subjection and danger. And now," said Sir Gawaine, "ye shall miss Sir Launcelot. But alas, I would not accord with him, and therefore," said Sir Gawaine, "I pray you, fair uncle, that I may have paper, pen and ink, that I may write to Sir Launcelot a letter with mine own hands."

And then when paper and ink was brought, Gawaine, who made a confession moments before, was set up weakly by King Arthur; and then he wrote thus, as the French book maketh mention: "Unto Sir Launcelot, flower of all noble knights that ever I heard of or saw by my days, I, Sir Gawaine, King Lot's son of Orkney, sister's son unto the noble King Arthur, send thee greeting, and let thee have knowledge that the tenth day of May I was smitten upon the old wound that thou gavest me before the city of Benwick, and through the same wound that thou gavest me I am come to my death day. And I will that all the world know, that I, Sir Gawaine, knight of the Table Round, sought my death, and not through thy deserving, but it was mine own seeking; wherefore I beseech thee, Sir Launcelot, to return again unto this realm, and see my tomb, and pray some prayer more or less for my soul. And this same day that I wrote this letter, I was hurt to death in the same wound, which I had of thy hand, Sir Launcelot; for of a more nobler man might I not be slain. Also Sir Launcelot, for all the love that ever was betwixt us, make no tarrying, but come over the sea in all haste, that thou mayst with thy noble knights rescue that noble king that made thee knight, that is my lord Arthur, for he is full straightly besieged by a false traitor, my half-brother, Sir Mordred; and he hath crowned himself king, and would have wedded my lady Queen Guenever, and would have had she not put herself in the Tower of London. And so on the tenth day of May last past, my lord Arthur and we all landed upon them at Dover; and there we put that false traitor, Sir Mordred, to flight, and there it misfortuned me to be stricken upon thy stroke. And this letter was written, but two hours and a half before my death, with mine own hand, and so subscribed with part of my heart's blood. And I require thee, most famous knight of the world, that thou wilt see my tomb."

And then Sir Gawaine wept, and King Arthur wept; and then they both swooned. And when they both awaked, the king made Sir Gawaine to receive his Savior. And then Sir Gawaine prayed for the king to send for Sir Launcelot, and to cherish him above all other knights. And so at the hour of noon, Sir Gawaine yielded up the spirit; and then the king interred him in a chapel within Dover Castle; and there still all men may see the skull of him, and the same wound is seen that Sir Launcelot gave him in battle. Then was it told the king that Sir Mordred had occupied a new field upon Barham Down. And upon the morn the king rode thither to challenge him, and there was a great battle betwixt them, and much people was slain on both parties. But at the last Sir Arthur's party stood best, and Sir Mordred and his party fled unto Canterbury.

How, after the battle, Sir Gawaine's ghost appeared to King Arthur and warned him that he should not fight that day.

And then the king searched all the towns for his knights that were slain, and interred them; and salved them with soft salves that were sorely wounded. Then much people drew unto King Arthur. And then they said that Sir Mordred warred upon King Arthur with wrong. And then King Arthur drew him with his host down by the seaside westward toward Salisbury, and there was a day assigned betwixt King Arthur and Sir Mordred, that they should meet upon a down beside Salisbury, and not far from the seaside; and this day was assigned on a Monday after Trinity Sunday, and King Arthur was passing glad that he might be avenged upon Sir Mordred. Then Sir Mordred gathered much people about London, for they of Kent, Southsex, and Surrey, Eastsex, and of Southfolk, and of Northfolk, held the most part with Sir Mordred; and many a full noble knight drew unto Sir Mordred and to the king. But they who loved Sir Launcelot drew unto Sir Mordred. So upon Trinity Sunday at night, King Arthur dreamed a wonderful dream, and that was this: he sat upon a platform in a chair, and the chair was fast to a wheel, and thereupon sat King Arthur in the richest cloth of gold that might be made; and the king thought there was under him, far from him, an hideous deep black water, and therein were all manner of serpents, and worms, and wild beasts, foul and horrible. And suddenly the king thought the wheel turned upside down, and he fell among the serpents, and every beast took him by a limb. And then the king cried, as he lay in his bed and slept, "Help." And then knights, squires, and yeomen awaked the king; and then he was so amazed that he knew not where he was; and then he started slumbering again, neither sleeping nor thoroughly waking. So the king seemed verily that there came Sir Gawaine unto him with a number of fair ladies with him. And when King Arthur saw him, then he said: "Welcome, my sister's son; I thought thou hadst been dead, and now I see thee alive—much am I beholding unto almighty Jesu. O fair nephew and my sister's son, what be these ladies that hither come with you?"

"Sir," said Sir Gawaine, "all these be ladies for whom I have fought when I was a living man, and all these are those that I did battle for in righteous quarrel; and God hath given them that grace at their great prayer, by cause I did battle for them, that they should bring me hither unto you: this much hath God given me leave, for to warn you of your death; for if ye fight tomorrow with Sir Mordred, as ye both have assigned, doubt ye not ye must be slain, and the most part of your people on both parties. And for the great grace and goodness that almighty Jesu hath unto you, and for pity of you, and many more other good men there shall be slain, God hath sent me to you of his special grace, to give you warning that in no wise do battle tomorrow, but that ye take a treaty for a month day; and proffer you largely, so that tomorrow be delayed. For within a month shall come Sir Launcelot with all his noble knights, and rescue you worshipfully, and slay Sir Mordred, and all that ever will hold with him."

Then Sir Gawaine and all the ladies vanished. And anon the king called upon his knights, squires, and yeomen, and charged them courageously to fetch his noble lords and wise bishops unto him. And when they were come, the king told them of his vision, of what Sir Gawaine had told him, and warned him that if he fought on the morn he should be slain. Then the king commanded Sir Lucan the Butler, and his brother Sir Bedivere, with two bishops with them, and charged them in any wise, as they might, to take a treaty for a month day to Sir Mordred, and to spare not, to offer him lands and goods as much as they thought necessary. So then they departed, and came to Sir Mordred, where he had a grim host of an hundred thousand men. And there they entreated Sir Mordred for a long time; and at last Sir Mordred was agreed for to have Cromwell and Kent, by Arthur's days: and after the days of King Arthur, all England.

How by misadventure of an adder the battle began, where Mordred was slain, and Arthur hurt to death.

Then were they condescended that King Arthur and Sir Mordred should meet betwixt both their hosts, and every each of them should bring fourteen persons; and they came with this word unto Arthur. Then said he: "I am glad that this is done." And so he went into the field. And when Arthur should depart, he warned all his host, that if they see any sword drawn, come on fiercely, and slay that traitor, Sir Mordred, "for I in no wise trust him." In likewise manner Sir Mordred warned his host: "If ye see any sword drawn, look that ye come on fiercely, and so slay all that ever before you standeth; for in no wise I will not trust for this treaty, for I know well my father wants to be avenged on me." And so they met as their appointment was, and so they were agreed and accorded thoroughly, and wine was fetched, and they drank. Right soon came an adder out of a little heath bush, and it stung a knight on the foot. And when the knight felt him stung, he looked down and saw the adder, and then drew his sword to slay the adder, and thought of none other harm. And when the host on both parties saw that sword drawn, then they blew bugles, trumpets, and horns, and shouted grimly. And so both armies came together.

And King Arthur took his horse, and said: "Alas this unhappy day!" And so rode to his party. And Sir Mordred did likewise. And never was there seen a more dolefuller battle in no Christian land; for there was but rushing and riding, foining and striking, and many a grim word was there spoken either to other, and many a deadly stroke. But ever King Arthur rode throughout the battle of Sir Mordred many times, and did full nobly as a noble king should, and at all times he fainted never; and Sir Mordred that day put him in trouble, and in great peril. And thus they fought all the long day, and never stinted till the noble knights were laid to the cold earth; and ever they fought still till it was near night, and by that time was there an hundred thousand laid dead upon the down. Then was Arthur mad and wroth out of measure, when he saw his people so slain from him. Then the king looked about him, and then was he ware, of all his host and of all his good knights, were left no more alive but two knights; that one was Sir Lucan the Butler, and his brother Sir Bedivere, and they were full sore wounded.

"Jesu mercy," said the king, "what became of all my noble knights? Alas that ever I should see this doleful day, for now," said Arthur, "I am come to mine end. But would to God that I knew where were that traitor Sir Mordred, that hath caused all this mischief." Then was King Arthur aware where Sir Mordred leaned upon his sword among a great heap of dead men. "Now give me my spear," said Arthur unto Sir Lucan, "for yonder I have espied the traitor that all this woe hath wrought."

"Sir, let him be," said Sir Lucan, "for he is unhappy; and if ye pass this unhappy day ye shall be right well revenged upon him. Good lord, remember ye of your night's dream, and what the spirit of Sir Gawaine told you this night, yet God of his great goodness hath preserved you hitherto. Therefore, for God's sake, my lord, leave off by this, for blessed be God ye have won the field, for here we be three alive, and with Sir Mordred is none alive; and if ye leave off now this wicked day of destiny is past."

"Tide me death, betide me life," saith the king, "now that I see him yonder alone he shall never escape mine hands, for at a better avail shall I never have him."

"God speed you well," said Sir Bedivere.

Then the king gat his spear in both his hands, and ran toward Sir Mordred crying: "Traitor, now is thy death day come." And when Sir Mordred heard Sir Arthur, he ran toward him with his sword drawn in his hand. And there King Arthur smote Sir Mordred under the shield, with a prong of his spear, throughout the body, more than a fathom. And when Sir Mordred felt that he had his death wound he thrust himself with all the might that he had up to the burr of King Arthur's spear. And right so he smote his father Arthur, with his sword holden in both his hands, on the side of the head, so that the sword pierced the helmet and the brain pan, and therewithal Sir Mordred fell stark dead to the earth; and the noble Arthur fell in a swoon to the earth, and there he swooned ofttimes. And Sir Lucan the Butler and Sir Bedivere ofttimes heaved him up. And so weakly they led him betwixt them both, to a little chapel not far from the seaside. And when the king was there he thought him well eased. Then heard they people cry in the field.

"Now go thou, Sir Lucan," said the king, "and do me to know what betokens that noise in the field." So Sir Lucan departed, for he was grievously wounded in many places. And so as he went, he saw and hearkened by the moonlight, how that pillers and robbers were come into the field, to pill and to rob many a full noble knight of brooches, and beads, of many a good ring, and of many a rich jewel; and those who were not dead they slew for their harness and their riches. When Sir Lucan understood this work, he came to the king as soon as he might, and told him all that he had heard and seen.

"Therefore by my counsel," said Sir Lucan, "it is best that we bring you to some town."

"I would it were so," said the king.

How King Arthur commanded to cast his sword Excalibur into the water, and how he was delivered to ladies in a barge.

"But I may not stand, mine head works so. Ah Sir Launcelot," said King Arthur, "this day have I sore missed thee; alas, that ever I was against thee, for now have I my death, whereof Sir Gawaine warned me in my dream." Then Sir Lucan took up the king by one arm, and Sir Bedivere by the other, and in the lifting the king swooned; and Sir Lucan fell in a swoon with the lift, and a part of his guts fell out of his body. And then the noble knight's heart burst. And when the king awoke, he beheld Sir Lucan, how he lay foaming at the mouth, and part of his guts lay at his feet.

"Alas," said the king, "this is to me a full heavy sight, to see this noble duke so die for my sake, for he would have helped me, who had more need of help than I. Alas, he would not complain, so set was his heart to help me: now Jesu have mercy upon his soul!" Then Sir Bedivere wept for the death of his brother. "Leave this mourning and weeping," said the king, "for all this will not avail me, for believe me if I lived myself, the death of Sir Lucan would grieve me evermore; but my time hieth fast," said the king.

"Therefore," said Arthur unto Sir Bedivere, "take thou Excalibur, my good sword, and go with it to yonder water side, and when thou comest there I charge thee throw my sword in that water, and come again and tell me what thou there seest."

"My lord," said Sir Bedivere, "your commandment shall be done, and lightly I will bring you word again." So Sir Bedivere departed, and by the way he beheld that noble sword, that the pommel and the shaft was all of precious stones; and then he said to himself: "If I throw this rich sword in the water, thereof shall never come good, but harm and loss." And then Sir Bedivere hid Excalibur under a tree. And so, as soon as he might, he came again unto the king, and said he had been at the water, and had thrown the sword in the water.

"What saw thou there?" said the king.

"Sir," he said, "I saw nothing but waves and winds."

"That is untruly said of thee," said the king, "therefore go thou lightly again, and do my commandment; as thou art to me life and breath, spare not, but throw it in." Then Sir Bedivere returned again, and took the sword in his hand; and then him thought it a sin and a shame to throw away that noble sword, and so again he hid the sword, and returned again, and told to the king that he had been at the water, and done his commandment.

"What saw thou there?" said the king.

"Sir," he said, "I saw nothing but the waters ebb and flow."

"Ah, traitor untrue," said King Arthur, "now hast thou betrayed me twice. Who would have guessed that, thou that hast been to me so true and dear? That thou who art named a noble knight would betray me for the richness of the sword. But now go again lightly, for thy long tarrying putteth me in great jeopardy of my life, for I have taken cold. And but if thou do now as I bid thee, if ever I may see thee, I shall slay thee with mine own hands; for thou wouldst for my rich sword see me dead." Then Sir Bedivere departed, and went to the sword, and lightly took it up, and went to the water side; and there he bound the girdle about the hilts, and then he threw the sword as far

134

into the water as he might; and there came an arm and an hand above the water and met it, and caught it, and so shook it thrice and brandished it. And then vanished away the hand with the sword in the water. So Sir Bedivere came again to the king, and told him what he saw.

"Alas," said the king, " help me hence, for I dread me I have tarried over long." Then Sir Bedivere took the king upon his back, and so went with him to that water side. And when they were at the water side, anchored by the bank was a little barge with many fair ladies in it, and among them all was a queen, and all they had black hoods, and all they wept and shrieked when they saw King Arthur.

"Now put me into the barge," said the king. And so he did softly; and there received him three queens in great mourning; and so they set them down, and in one of their laps King Arthur laid his head. And then that queen said: "Ah, dear brother, why have ye tarried so long from me? Alas, this wound on your head hath caught over-much cold." And so then they rowed from the land, and Sir Bedivere beheld all those ladies go from him.

Then Sir Bedivere cried: "Ah, my lord Arthur, what shall become of me, now ye go from me and leave me here alone among mine enemies?"

"Comfort thyself," said the king, "and do as well as thou mayest, for in me is no trust for to trust in; for I will into the vale of Avilion to heal me of my grievous wound: and if thou hear never more of me, pray for my soul." But ever the queens and ladies wept and shrieked, that it was a pity to hear. And as soon as Sir Bedivere had lost the sight of the barge, he wept and wailed, and so took to the forest. And so he traveled all that night, and in the morning became aware, betwixt two gnarled trees, of a chapel and an hermitage.

How Sir Bedivere found him on the morrow dead in an hermitage, and how he abode there with the hermit.

Then was Sir Bedivere glad, and thither he went; and when he came into the chapel, he saw where lay an hermit groveling on all fours, next to a tomb newly dug. When the hermit saw Sir Bedivere he knew him well, for he was but a little before Bishop of Canterbury, that Sir Mordred put to flight.

"Sir," said Bedivere, "what man is there interred that ye pray so fast for?"

"Fair son," said the hermit, "I know not verily, but can guess.

"This night, at midnight, here came a number of ladies, and brought hither a dead corpse, and prayed me to bury him; and here they offered an hundred tapers, and they gave me an hundred besants."

"Alas," said Sir Bedivere, "that was my lord King Arthur, that here lieth buried in this chapel." Then Sir Bedivere swooned; and when he awoke he prayed to the hermit that he might abide with him there, to live with fasting and prayers.

"For from hence will I never go," said Sir Bedivere, "by my will, but all the days of my life pray here for my lord Arthur."

"Ye are welcome to me," said the hermit, "for I knew ye better than ye think I do. Ye are the bold Bedivere, and the full noble duke, Sir Lucan the Butler, was your brother." Then Sir Bedivere told the hermit all as ye have heard. So there dwelt Sir Bedivere with the hermit that was previously Bishop of Canterbury, and there Sir Bedivere put upon him poor clothes, and served the hermit full lowly in fasting and in prayers. Thus of Arthur I find never more written in books that be authorized, nor more of the very certainty of death, but thus was he led away in a ship wherein were three queens; that one was King Arthur's sister, Queen Morgan le Fay; the other was the Queen of Northgalis; the third was the Queen of the Waste Lands. Also there was Nimue, the chief lady of the lake, that had wedded Pelleas the good knight; and this lady had done much for King Arthur, for she would never suffer Sir Pelleas to be in no place where he should be in danger of his life; and so he lived to the uttermost of his days with her in great rest. More of the death of King Arthur could I never find, but that ladies brought him to his burials; and such one was buried there, that the hermit bore witness that sometime was Bishop of Canterbury, but yet the hermit knew not in certain that he was verily the body of King Arthur; for this tale Sir Bedivere, knight of the Table Round, made it to be written.

Of the opinion of some men of the death of King Arthur; and how Queen Guenever made her a nun in Almesbury.

Yet some men say in many parts of England that King Arthur is not dead, but had gone by the will of our Lord Jesu into another place; and men say that he shall come again, and he shall win the holy cross. I will not say it shall be so, but rather I will say, here in this world he changed his life. But many men say there is written upon his tomb this verse: "Here lies Arthur, the once and future king." Thus leave I here Sir Bedivere with the hermit, that dwelled that time in a chapel beside Glastonbury, and there was his hermitage. And so they lived in their prayers, and fastings, and great abstinence. And when Queen Guenever understood that King Arthur was slain, and all the noble knights, Sir Mordred, and all the remnant, then the queen stole away, and five ladies with her, and so she went to Almesbury; and there she let make herself a nun, and wore white clothes and black, and great penance she took, as ever did sinful lady in this land, and never creature could make her merry. She lived in fasting, prayers, and alms-deeds, so that all manner of people marveled how virtuously she had changed.

# Eliduc

*Infidelity, innocence and self-sacrifice form an almost irresolvable triangle in this, the longest and most enigmatic of the lais of Marie de France, the western tradition's first major woman writer.*

any knights served the king of Brittany, but none was more valiant and courtly, more courageous and proud, than Eliduc. Time and again, Eliduc volunteered his services, protected the king's land. But envy among his fellow knights started rumors, and a day never passed when jealous peers didn't urge their king to exile Eliduc. The knight tried to justify himself, begged the king to listen to his defense, but finally, in despair, he called his friends together.

"The king is expelling me from his court," said Eliduc, "and I shan't speak of how many ways, until this day, I served him with all my loyalty. Perhaps the peasant proverb is right: 'Never argue with your workhorse, never count on the recognition of your prince.'"

He said, "I am leaving you now to journey to the kingdom of Logres, across the sea, and I shall bring with me only d'Yvain, the faithful bearer of my armor. My wife will remain here, to care for my land, and I beg you to protect her and give her your advice while I'm gone."

Dressed in his finest clothes, Eliduc took leave of his friends and took his wife, Guildeluec, in his arms, promising to keep his love for her, to be faithful. Eliduc left the court, accompanied by d'Yvain.

On horses they reached the sea, where they boarded a ship that crossed the sea and arrived in the kingdom of Logres, which had been devastated by war. Eliduc immediately offered his services to the old and ancient king, and in the king's battles he fought in the midst of the knights, his sword in his hand. The king had a marriageable daughter, whose hand his enemy wanted. At first Eliduc lived in the city, at the home of a very wealthy, very wise citizen, who lent Eliduc his loveliest rooms. Eliduc took his ease there, and often invited the poorest knights to dinner. One day, in the course of a bloody battle, Eliduc discovered the intentions of the enemy, outwitted them, and captured their leader. Peace quickly returned to the kingdom.

Guilliardon, the king's beautiful daughter, became curious about this hero all the courtiers praised for his courage and wisdom. She sent her most trustworthy chamberlain to summon Eliduc, who was entering the castle courtyard on horseback when the messenger reached him and told him the princess wished to receive him, in her rooms, at once. When he entered her private chamber, Eliduc thanked Guilliardon profusely. Blushing, she invited him to sit at her side, on her bed. In uninterrupted conversation their lips spoke of a thousand and one things, while the god of love shot his arrows. From looking at him the beautiful princess went pale and sighed, and Eliduc noticed. Finally, he took his leave (manners did not permit too long a first meeting), and the princess was conscience-stricken.

"Alas, I see this knight for the first time; I pay no attention to who he is, no mind where he comes from; and yet I love him already. Now that the kingdom is returned to peace he will no doubt leave here to follow his path to honor elsewhere. My path will be despair. Should I reveal to him my feelings? Has he such kindness not to blame me for them?"

She passed the night without sleep, caught up in thoughts and monologues in which the name of Eliduc echoed and re-echoed. At dawn she called her nurse and confided her troubles.

"By my faith, my only confidant, I love my father's new knight; and I, the heiress of the king, plan to ask him to give me his love. One day he will be king of Logres, and on our heads we too will carry the kingdom's crown. If he doesn't want my advances, doesn't love me with real love, I shall die of sorrow."

"Mistress, you have no reason to despair — many are the kings attracted by your beauty. But since your heart is captured by this knight, give me a token, a belt or a ring, and I will give it to him as a sign of friendship. Surely he will not refuse it."

"So be it. I will give you an embroidered belt and a gold ring; take them to him. I hope he doesn't fine me audacious or ridiculous; but even if he does it doesn't matter, because I love him."

During this time Eliduc, in his room, found himself prey to troubled thoughts. Guilliardon's beauty deeply moved him, but he had promised his wife he would remain faithful to her.

Guilliardon's chamberlain arrived at Eliduc's room, greeted him, and presented the princess's gifts. The knight accepted them, putting the gold ring on his finger and tying the embroidered belt tightly around his waist as the messenger left quietly. She hastened to rejoin her mistress and tell her the good news. Eliduc, for his part, grew impatient to see the princess again, anxious to have his next meal in the royal palace. He joined the king again in Guilliardon's rooms, where a knight recently returned from Asia was teaching her to play chess.

"My beauty," said the king to his daughter, "be kind to our young heroes." All smiles, the princess took Eliduc aside from the others. They sat down, letting their glances declare that they were in love. The knight thanked the princess for the presents, and she agreed to accept his hand. At this, blaming himself for being unfaithful to Guildeluec, who waited for him at home in Brittany, he became so upset he could scarcely speak any more of love. And moments later, a messenger from the king of Brittany arrived, asking Eliduc to return to his court because the jealous knights who had slandered him had all been exiled, and the king needed his help. But here, even as he announced he must leave, repledge his loyalty to his king, was this woman other than his wife who told him her joy at knowing he would soon return, which he promised to do.

"Alas," said Eliduc to himself, "if only I didn't have to leave this country. For my sins and the love that united me to this beautiful princess will never be realized — because I am married."

Shortly thereafter he went to the king and said to him:

"Sire, I have received a message from my first master, the king of Brittany, who wishes that I return. Now that peace has returned to your kingdom, I ask your leave to answer his call."

Saddened, the king wasn't able to refuse this favor to the one who had been his greatest help; and he even tried to give Eliduc many gifts: gold, dogs, horses, the finest silk. But Eliduc refused them, saying he would find all these riches when he returned to his country, and expressing only a desire to bid the princess farewell before leaving. Once they were alone, Guilliardon felt the pain of Eliduc's departure. She fell into a swoon from grief. The knight had no time to prevent her fall, but he wrapped his arms around her and his eyes filled with tears. He covered her with kisses. More and more passionately he kissed her lips, and at the moment she opened her eyes, his voice was saying to her:

"My sweet, I want to return to my country, help my noble king, but, my life and my death, I do not want to leave you. A cruel necessity leaves me helpless."

"Why not ask my father, the king, to permit me to go with you? He will not be able to refuse you after all your exploits, after all you've done for his kingdom."

"Alas, I am only a poor knight, without inheritance, and your father will, and rightfully, refuse me such a request."

"I don't believe that. I have no desire to live without you. Take me with you or I will kill myself."

Eliduc, surprised by so much passion, decided to take her with him, and enlisted the help of his armor-bearer, d'Yvain.

" d'Yvain," he said, "I have every respect for you, think of you as my right arm, and I know I can count on your discretion when I ask you not to mention my wife in front of Guilliardon. The princess will join us tonight at the edge of the forest beside the lake. She will go with us to Brittany."

"Is this possible?" said d'Yvain, the noble armor-bearer.

"You cannot understand this, but promise me to speak no more of it."

"But, sire, how can I forget the goodness that your wife, Guildeluec, who waits for you in Brittany, showed this poor armor-bearer that I am?" answered d'Yvain.

"That doesn't matter. Give me your promise of faithfulness and silence," demanded Eliduc.

"I give it."

When night and darkness came Guilliardon secretly left the royal palace, dressed in a silk gown embroidered with gold, her face hidden by a cloak. She reached the forest beside the lake, an arrow's shot from the castle, and found there her lover, impatiently waiting with his armor-bearer. They reached the port without delay. When their boat neared the shores of Britanny a fierce storm boiled the sea, preventing them from safely landing. On the ship there was only desolation, and in their distress the three navigators addressed strong prayers to Saint Nicholas, Saint Clement, and the Virgin Mary. But their prayers seemed in vain, and the winds redoubled their force. Taken by fear, d'Yvain, who had little courage in his heart but only love for his master, cried:

"Sire, we have the cause of our misfortunes on board, the woman for whom you have perjured yourself, the woman who made you forget the loyal Guildeluec who waits for you in Brittany, your wife. Why not throw her overboard? Isn't that the way to get a favorable wind?"

Eliduc answered angrily:

"Didn't you promise me never to mention my wife? And now you want me to murder my sweetheart."

Guilliardon, who had missed none of this conversation, for the first time realized her lover had a wife, and fell over in a swoon so profound Eliduc thought her dead. In his despair he grabbed an oar and hit his armor-bearer with so much force that d'Yvain fell dead on the spot. Then, anxious to get rid of the body, he grasped d'Yvain's corpse by the feet and threw it overboard. Waves carried the body away.

Eliduc manned the ship's rudder, and under his direction the boat made it into port. They left the raging elements for shelter. Eliduc could not believe that all life had left Guilliardon's body, which even in death looked rosy. He remembered that in the neighborhood, in the depths of a great forest, there lived a holy hermit he had known well in his youth.

"I will take the body of Guilliardon to the hermit for his blessing, and for myself I will make a confession and be purified. Then we will bury my dead sweetheart in the chapel, and I will give the holy man so much money that he will be able to found an abbey, where the monks will pray all day for the repose of her soul, for the soul of she who died of love."

With his sad burden, Eliduc arrived at the hermitage, only to be astonished when no one answered his knocks on the door. He lay the body on the grass and, after climbing the wall, leaped into the enclosure. By the light of the moon he discovered the tomb of the hermit. Faced with this unexpected situation, he didn't know what to do. Should he open the tomb? Where could he find the tools? He carried the body into the chapel, put it before the altar, and gave himself up to despair.

"Friend," he said to his dead sweetheart, "unhappy was the hour when I met you, and when you decided to love me. Your beauty gave you, by my troth, an enviable future as a grand kingdom's queen. My fate is a wretched one, and I will retire to a monastery, where in silence and holy prayer I will live out my sad life in memory of your love."

Throwing himself on the lifeless body, Eliduc gave vent for hours to his suffering, until the moment when duty bid him leave the hermitage and join his wife, who had been waiting for him so long in Brittany. She greeted him with joy, but the absence of d'Yvain worried her. Eliduc, to calm her, told the story of the storm at sea, during the course of which, he said, a vicious wave swept the faithful armor-bearer into the sea.

After returning to his country, Eliduc led a life that seemed somewhat strange to his wife and friends—he wished only for silence, and avoided all company. After morning mass he disappeared, until night, into the forest's depths. There, not noticing her pallor for her beauty, he prayed before the altar, by the body of Guilliardon. He would stay there until twilight, oblivious to the song of birds, the many noises of the forest.

Guildeluec was worried by the silences and the long absences of her husband, and she spoke to a faithful servant, begging him to follow her husband, to find out where he went each day.

"After mass you will find me under the trees. Come tell me where my husband goes each day and I will reward you generously."

The servant followed the steps of Eliduc into the forest's depths, where, at the chapel door, he heard his master's cries. He returned to his mistress.

"How can this be, my husband in tears?" she said. "That astonishes me, and even though I know Eliduc had deep affection for the hermit, may he rest in peace, I am not able to explain this conduct. He has to remain in court all day tomorrow; while he's occupied, you must take me to the hermitage."

The next day Eliduc returned to courtly business while Guildeluec went to the chapel. What was her astonishment to see the body lying on the flagstones? She turned back the sheet covering the body, and discovered a face so beautiful that it explained her husband's absences. She called the servant, and said to him calmly and serenely:

"This is the body of a friend of Eliduc's, and now I understand his grief. She is so beautiful that I do not wish to part them."

At that moment a weasel ran out from under the altar and passed over the body of Guilliardon. The servant chased it and struck it with a stick, and the weasel lay dead on the ground. The excitement caused another weasel to emerge from beneath the altar, and the second weasel tried in vain to revive its dead mate. The weasel left the chapel, went to a neighboring field, and with her fangs picked a red flower and placed it in the mouth of her dead mate. Instantly, the weasel came back to life. Then both weasels fled. Surprised, Guildeluec took the flower and placed it between the lips of the unconscious beauty. The color rushed back to her cheeks, her eyes opened, and, as if recovering from a deep sleep, Guilliardon said:

"Heavens, I've slept a long time."

Guildeluec came closer to her and asked her where her home was.

"I am the daughter of the king of Logres, and I came to know Eliduc, a brave knight who was valiant in service to my father. I loved him very much, and desired to come with him when he returned to his country. But oh, unhappy me, he sinned and deceived me. I discovered one day that he already had a wife, and in the shock of that knowledge I fell into a faint. Where am I now? What will become of me in this strange country, alone in a gloomy forest?"

"My dear," answered Guildeluec, "I am the wife of Eliduc, and I can assure you that my husband's feelings toward you have not changed. His love for you is extremely strong, and there is never a day when he cannot be found in despair because he believes you dead. Now I understand his silence and his long absences, why he has so often left me alone. It is only because I wanted to discover the secret of his unhappiness that I found you, and that you have come back to life gives me great joy. Follow me and I will take you to your sweetheart, at once, without resentment. For a long time I have wanted to dedicate myself to a life of prayer and retire to a cloister. I shall do that now, rather than force you two to part."

Reassured by this friendly attitude on the part of her rival, Guilliardon rose and followed her to the home of the knight. Eliduc, whose servant told him of the miracle, took into his arms Guilliardon, from whom he had thought himself forever parted. His wife, watching the scene closely, said to Eliduc:

"I understand your joy and do not feel any resentment. I am going to enter a convent and you will be able to marry your sweetheart."

Feeling the greatest respect for this decision by his wife, who had always been pious, Eliduc built a rich abbey around the hermitage, with beautiful gardens and a rich endowment. There Guildeluec established a convent with about thirty nuns, and Eliduc celebrated his second marriage.

For a while, it seemed that the sacrifice of Guildeluec had attracted, both to the cloister and to the newly married couple, the blessing of heaven. In her prayers, in the superior life of friendship, in her respect for her comrades, Guildeluec forgot her previous life and her turbulent marriage. She found a blessed peace for her soul in the vows of the church, and in the silence of her cell.

Many happy and fruitful seasons passed, peaceful and secure, and just as the kingdom flourished, so did Eliduc and Guilliardon's love. Each night and each morning they prayed for their love and for the love of Guildeluec, who had sacrificed her worldly life to ensure it, and who prayed each day, as they did, that their love would last forever.

Gradually, Eliduc and Guilliardon's love grew too vast for them to understand, and with each season they turned more and more toward God. They gave great alms to all the needy, fertile lands to loyal serfs and poor farmers, and one spring day, when the dewdrops gleamed in the sun like diamonds, Eliduc said to his love:

"My life, my death, my angel of this world, our love is too great, too vast for just ourselves. I shall distribute my land among my noblest vassals, and I shall build a rich church at the forest's edge. I shall give my life to God in the name of our love, and I shall entrust you to the faultless Guildeluec, whose love made our love possible, who sacrificed her love for ours."

From his church each day Eliduc sent letters to Guilliardon and Guildeluec, and each day they sent letters to him. All three went to great pains to show their love for each other, and their love for God.

The ancient Britons wrote down this tale, so none would ever forget.

# The Knight of the Swan

*This tale combines several popular elements of medieval narrative
— magical births, a wicked widow and the transformation of
humans into animals.*

 ing Pieron and Queen Matabrune had a son, Oriant, who
reigned after his father died, living in the palace with his
widowed mother. One day, hunting in the forest, King
Oriant lost his way, and while resting by a fountain met a
party comprising a young damsel of a noble but sad
demeanor escorted by a knight with two squires and three ladies in waiting.
Oriant wooed and eventually married this lady, Beatrice, much to the
dismay and enmity of his mother Matabrune, who found herself displaced
in the palace.

Shortly afterward, Oriant was called away to war, and he entrusted
Beatrice to the care of his mother. The time came for Beatrice, who was
pregnant, to be delivered, and her false mother-in-law prepared a wicked
plan. In great pain and labor Beatrice bore six sons and a fair daughter, each
having a chain of silver about their necks as they issued out of their mother's
womb. When Matabrune saw the seven children born, each having a chain
of silver at the neck, she had them secretly taken aside by a chambermaid
who was under her influence and took seven little pups that she had prepared, and laid them all bloody under the queen as if they had issued from
her body.

Matabrune ordered her squire to drown the seven children in the river, but in compassion he left them in the forest, wrapped in his cloak, where a hermit found them, nurtured them and baptized them, calling the most beautiful of the boys Helias. One day these children were seen in the forest, all with silver chains round their necks, by a servant of Matabrune who reported it immediately to the queen mother, and she again gave orders for the children to be slaughtered. But the hired assassins found only six children — the hermit having taken Helias on a begging excursion — and they spared the infants, only robbing them of their silver chains. As soon as their chains were off, they were all changed in an instant to fair white swans by divine grace, and they began to fly in the air over the forest making piteous and lamentable cries.

Helias grew up with his godfather in the forest. In a vision, the hermit was told whose children these were by an angel. At the palace Matabrune's campaign of malice against Beatrice was finally succeeding, and a false charge was brought against the queen. But Helias was by now a young man, and as Beatrice was about to be executed he appeared in the lists, and by his valor proclaimed her innocence and confounded Matabrune's plans.

Helias, reunited with his father, Oriant, asked for the silver chains that had been taken from his brothers and sister, and swore that he would never rest until he had found the swans and returned their chains to them. He did find them, and they recognized him at once, and came lightly fawning and fluttering about him, giving him cheer. To five of them Helias restored the chains, and they returned to their human form. But the sixth chain had been melted to make a silver goblet, and one of the brothers was unable to regain his human shape.

One day in L'Ile Fort, Helias saw this swan, his brother, drawing a ship to the wharf, and he took it as a sign that he should go by the guiding of the swan into some far country to seek his honor and his fate. He took leave of his family with great ceremony and sailed away in the ship drawn by the swan.

At this time, Otho, emperor of Germany, held court at Neumagen to decide a claim by the count of Frankfort for the duchy of Bouillon, then held by Clarissa as duchess of Bouillon. The claim was to be decided by single combat, and Duchess Clarissa sought a champion to fight the count of

Frankfort. God sent Helias's ship sailing up the Meuse at the time, led by the swan who drew the craft by a silver chain. Helias championed Clarissa, won the battle, married her and became Duke of Bouillon. Before the marriage he warned the lady that if she ever asked his name or his origins he would have to leave her.

Helias and Clarissa had a number of children, including Godfrey de Bouillon, later king of Jerusalem. One night Clarissa forgot her husband's warning and began to ask him about his name and kindred. He rebuked her sorrowfully and, leaving his bed, bade her farewell. At dawn the swan reappeared on the river, drawing the little boat after it, and uttering loud cries to call his brother. Helias stepped into the boat, and the swan took it out of the sight of the sorrowful lady, never to return.

# The Dean and the Magician

*This tale was written by Prince Juan Mauel Manuel of Spain in the 14th century. Like most of the writing in his work* Count Lucanor *it is written to present a specific moral lesson.*

**T**here was once a dean of Santiago who had a great desire to be initiated in the art of necromancy; and, hearing that Don Illan of Toledo knew more of this art than any other person in that country, came to Toledo with the hope of studying under him. On the day of his arrival he proceeded to the house of Don Illan, whom he found reading in his private chambers, and who received him very graciously, asking him not to inform him of the motive of his visit until he had first partaken of a meal, which he found excellent, and which consisted of every delicacy that could be desired.

Now, when the repast was concluded, the dean took the magician aside and told him the motive of his visit, urging him very earnestly to instruct him in the art in which he was so accomplished, and to which the dean desired so anxiously to be made an initiate.

When Don Illan told him that he was a dean and, consequently, a man of great influence, and that with his help he would attain a high position — saying, at the same time, that men, when they reach an elevated position and attain the objects of their ambition, generally forget what others have previously done for them, as well as their past obligations and their former promises — the dean assured him such should not be the case with him, and that no matter what eminence he might attain, he would not fail to do everything in his power to help his former friends, and the magician in particular.

In this way they conversed until suppertime approached; and now, the covenant between them being completed, Don Illan told the dean that, in teaching him the art he desired to learn, it would be necessary for them to retire to some distant chamber. As they were quitting the dining room, he called his housekeeper, desiring her to procure some partridges for their supper that night, but not to cook them until she had his special commands. Having said this, he conducted the dean to the entrance of a beautifully carved stone staircase, which they descended for a considerable distance. It appeared as if they had passed under the river and, arriving at the bottom of the steps, they found a suite of rooms and a very elegant chamber, in which were arranged the magician's books and instruments of study. Having seated themselves, they were debating which should be the first books to read, when two men entered by the door and gave the dean a letter that had been sent to him by his uncle the archbishop, informing him that he was dangerously ill, and that if he wished to see him alive it would be necessary for him to come immediately. The dean was much upset by this news — partly on account of the illness of his uncle, but more through fear of being obliged to abandon his favorite study, just commenced — so he wrote a respectful letter to his uncle the archbishop, which he sent by the same messengers. At the end of four days, other men arrived on foot bringing fresh letters to the dean, informing him that the archbishop was dead, and that all those interested in the welfare of the church were desirous that he should succeed his late uncle's position, telling him at the same time that it was quite unnecessary for him to inconvenience himself by returning immediately, as his nomination would be better secured were he not present in the church. At the end of seven or eight days, two squires arrived, very richly dressed and accoutred, who, after kissing his hand, delivered to him the letters informing him that he had been appointed archbishop.

When Don Illan heard this he told him he was much pleased that this good news had arrived during his stay in his house; and, as God had been so gracious to him, begged that the deanery might be given to his son.

The archbishop-elect replied that he hoped Don Illan would allow him to name the vacancy to his own brother, saying that he would present him with some office in his own church with which his son would be contented, inviting, at the same time, both father and son to accompany him to Santiago.

All three departed for the city, where they were received with much honor. After they had resided there some time, there arrived one day messengers from the pope bearing letters naming the former dean Bishop of Tolosa, permitting him at the same time to name whom he pleased to succeed him in his vacant see.

When Don Illan heard this he reminded him of his promise, urging him to confer the appointment on his son. But the archbishop again desired that the magician would allow him to name one of his paternal uncles to succeed him. Don Illan replied that, although he felt he was unjustly treated, he would reply on the future accomplishment of his promise. The archbishop thanked him, once again renewed his promise of future services, and, inviting Don Illan and his son to accompany him, set out for Tolosa, where they were well received by the counts and great men of the country.

They had resided there about two years when messengers again came from the pope with letters in which he announced to the archbishop that he had named him cardinal, allowing him, as before, to name his successor.

On this occasion Don Illan went to him, arguing that many vacancies had taken place, and that now he could plead no excuse; and urged the cardinal to confer this last dignity on his son. But once more the cardinal requested Don Illan to forgive his having bestowed the vacant see on one of his maternal uncles, saying he was a very good old man. He then proposed they should now depart for Rome, where undoubtedly he would do for them all they could desire. Don Illan complained very much, but nevertheless consented to accompany the cardinal to Rome. On their arrival they were very well received by the other cardinals and the entire court, and they lived there a long time. Don Illan daily importuned the cardinal to confer some appointment on his son, but the cardinal always found some excuse for not doing so.

While they were yet at Rome, the pope died, and all the cardinals assembled in conclave and elected our cardinal pope.

Then Don Illan came to him, saying, "You have now no excuse to offer for not fulfilling the promises you have made to me."

But the new pope told him not to bother him so much, as there was still time to think of him and his son.

Don Illan now began to complain in earnest. "You have," said he, "made me many promises, not one of which you have performed." He then recalled to his mind how earnestly the pope had pledged his word at their first interview to do all he could to help him, and as yet, had done nothing. "I have no longer any faith in your words," said Don Illan, "nor do I now expect anything from you."

These words angered the pope greatly, and he replied sharply, "If I am again annoyed in this manner I will have you thrown into prison as a heretic and a sorcerer. I know well that in Toledo, where you lived, you had no other means of support but by practicing the art of necromancy."

When Don Illan saw how ill the pope had treated him for what he had done, he prepared to depart, the pope refusing even to grant him the wherewithal to support himself on the road. "Then," he said to the pope, "since I have nothing to eat, I must needs fall back upon the partridges I ordered for tonight's supper." He then called out to his housekeeper, and ordered her to cook the birds for his supper.

No sooner had he spoken than the dean found himself again in Toledo, still dean of Santiago, as on his arrival, but so overwhelmed with shame that he knew not what to say.

"How fortunate it is," said Don Illan to him, "that I have thus proved the true value of your promises in prosperity; for, as it is, I should have considered it a great misfortune had I allowed you to partake of the partridges."

And so it is said:

> Who pays thy kindness with ungratefulness,
> The more he has to give, he'll give the less.

# Andreuccio, The Young Merchant

*This is the fifteenth tale in Boccaccio's* Decameron. *While the humor is at the expense of the ignorant hero, Boccaccio kindly lets him end his misadventure on a happy note.*

here was once a young man from Perugia, whose name was Andreuccio di Pietro, who dealt in fast horses. Hearing that horses were going for a song in Naples, he stuffed five hundred gold florins into his purse and in the company of some other merchants set off for that town. He'd never been away from home before. He arrived on Sunday evening toward vespers and, following his host's advice, went off to the market the next morning. There were plenty of horses, but although many of them took his fancy and he bargained for them, he never reached a definite agreement. However, to show that he really did intend to buy, every so often, like the fool he was, he brandished his purse of florins, regardless of who was passing by. A Sicilian woman, who was beautiful, but any man's for a price, noticed this purse as she was passing by. Careful not to let herself be seen, she said to herself:

"I'd like to get my hands on that purse. It could do me a lot of good!"

There was an old woman with this handsome woman, also a Sicilian, who, when she saw Andreuccio, let her companion walk on while she ran up to him and embraced him affectionately. When the handsome woman saw this, she stepped to one side to wait for her and didn't say a word. Andreuccio turned to the old woman and, recognizing her, gave her a warm welcome. She promised to visit him at his inn, and took her leave without chatting for very long. Andreuccio went back to his bartering but bought nothing that morning. The woman who had first noticed Andreuccio's purse, and then the old woman's acquaintance with him, made some discreet inquiries about the man, looking for a way to get her hands on the money. She asked who he was, and where he came from, what he did, and how she came to know him. The old woman told her everything about Andreuccio's business. She went into such detail that he might have been relating it himself. She explained that she had lodged with his father, first in Sicily and later in Perugia. She told her where he was staying and the purpose of his visit.

The woman, armed with this information regarding his name and parentage, sought to put a cunning plan into operation to get what she wanted. When they reached home she set the old woman so much work to do that she wouldn't have time to see Andreuccio that day. Then she summoned a maid, who had her confidence, and sent her toward evensong to the inn where Andreuccio was staying. As luck would have it, he answered the door himself and told the maid who he was. When she heard this she drew him to one side and said:

"Sir, with respect, there is a gentlewoman of this city who must speak with you."

When Andreuccio heard this he admired himself from head to toe. He liked what he saw, and thought he must be the only fine-looking fellow in all of Naples for the lady in question to have fallen in love with him. So without further ado he told the girl he was ready and asked when and where the lady would speak to him. The girl replied:

"Sir, if it's convenient, she is waiting in her house now."

Without a word to any of the others in the inn, Andreuccio replied immediately:

"You go on ahead and I will follow you."

Thus the girl brought him to her mistress's house, which was in a street known as Malpertugio, and that name in itself indicated just how remarkable the quarter was! He, however, knew nothing of these things, suspected nothing, and thought he was going to a respectable place to see a lady of quality. Thus, he entered the house without hesitation while the maid went in ahead of him, calling out to her mistress:

"Andreuccio is here."

Then she went up the stairs as the lady came to the head of the stairs to receive him. The lady was a tall young woman with fine features, and dressed in the most elegant way. As he went to meet her, she came down three steps and welcomed him with open arms. She threw her arms around his neck and wordlessly stayed like that as though overcome by a surfeit of tender emotion. Then she kissed him on the forehead, wept, and in a trembling voice said:

"O my Andreuccio, you are so welcome!"

He was amazed at such tender caresses, and in some confusion answered:

"Madam, the pleasure is mine."

Hearing this, she took him by the hand and brought him first to her drawing room; without saying another word, they then proceeded to her chamber, which was full of roses and orange flowers and exotically scented. Here he saw a very fine bed with curtains around it, dresses hanging from pegs, and all kinds of rich fine things common to those parts. Bumpkin that he was, this made him believe that she was indeed a great lady. She made him sit next to her on a chest at the bottom of the bed and explained herself to him:

"Andreuccio, I know you are surprised by my caresses and my tears, as anyone would be who didn't know me and had never heard of me, but you are in for an even greater shock: I am your sister. I can tell you this now since God has granted me the sight of one of my brothers — though I'd love to see you all before I die. However, I shall not die unhappy now. Let me explain.

"Pietro, your father and mine, as I'm sure you know, used to live in Palermo. He was much loved and admired there for his fine looks and sense of humor. He had many lovers, but the one who touched him most of all was my mother. She was a lady of good family, and then she became a widow. She put aside all fear of her father and brothers, not to mention her own honor, and was intimate with him. As a result, I was born and grew into the woman you see before you. Soon after this he left Palermo for Perugia and left me, just a little girl, with my mother. We never heard of him again. If it weren't for the fact that he was my father, I would despise him. He showed

no gratitude to my mother and no respect for me, his daughter, who wasn't born of a servant or person of low breeding. My mother, without knowing better and acting out of a very faithful love, gave him all her possessions and herself. But what good does it do to talk like this? What is past is past. But that was what happened.

"After he left, I grew up in Palermo, and when I was fully grown my mother, who was a wealthy woman, gave my hand to a worthy gentleman from Girgenti. Out of love for her and myself, he came to live in Palermo. Because he was a great Guelph, he made a treaty with our own King Charles. But before this could come into effect King Frederick got wind of it and we were forced to flee from Sicily, where I would have been the greatest lady that ever lived there. We took just a few things with us; I say few bearing in mind what we had. We left our lands and palaces and took refuge in this city. Here we found King Charles so moved by our loyal services that in part he made up for the losses we had suffered on his behalf. He gave us land and houses, and to this day provides my husband, your own relative, with a good living, as you will shortly see. This is how I come to be in this city, where, God have mercy and no thanks to you, my dear brother, you come to see me." Having said all this, she embraced him again and again, kissed him on the forehead, and wept with tenderness.

When Andreuccio heard this story, told as it was with such cunning that the lady hadn't stammered or faltered over a word, he remembered that his father had in fact been in Palermo. He also knew the ways of young men himself and how easily they fell in love in their youth. These facts coupled with the affectionate tears, embraces, and modest kisses convinced him that what she said was true. When she calmed down, he said:

"Madam, you must not be put out by my great surprise. To tell you the truth, my father, for whatever reason, never spoke of your mother or yourself. If he did, it certainly never came to my notice. I knew nothing of your existence, and it's therefore all the more dear to me to find you, my sister, here in this city, where I am alone and could hardly have expected this. Indeed, I know no one of such rank, that you should not be respected by them. I say nothing of myself, because I'm only a small-time trader. However, there's something I'm not clear about—how did you know I was here?"

To this she replied:

"A poor woman who frequently attends me told me about your arrival this morning. She told me that she used to live with our father in Palermo and Perugia. When I heard this I thought it only fitting that you should visit me in my own house rather than that I should go to another's house."

After this, she asked after the family by name, and he answered her and was even more convinced that what she said was true.

It was a hot day and they had spoken for some time, so the lady then called for some Greek wine and sweetmeats. She told Andreuccio to drink, and he would after that have taken his leave, as it was suppertime, but she wouldn't hear of it. She made a show of being annoyed and embraced him and said:

"Ah, I see now how little I mean to you! Who would believe that you meet a sister you've never seen before, you come to her house, and then you leave her to go and dine in a tavern? You must dine with me. My husband is abroad, a fact which distresses me, but you will receive every courtesy a woman has to offer."

Andreuccio, not really knowing what else to say, replied:

"I consider you dearly as a sister should be, but if I don't go I'll be considered rude because I am expected to supper."

"Good Lord," she said, "you would think I had no one in the house to send and tell them not to expect you! You'd do far better and be more dutiful if you invited your company to supper here. After that you could all go away together."

Andreuccio replied that he had no real desire to see his companions that evening and if it was agreeable to her, he would willingly stay. She then made a great show of sending to the inn to say that he was not to be expected to supper. After more talk they sat down to eat and were sumptuously served with different kinds of meat while she skillfully spun out the meal until it was dark. They then left the table, and Andreuccio would have taken his leave but she wouldn't hear of it. Naples, she explained, was no place to go about at night, especially if you were a stranger. In fact, when she sent to the inn to say that he would not come for supper she had informed them that he would also be out for the night. Andreuccio believed all this and took pleasure in being with her. He was fooled by her story and thus stayed where he was. After supper, they spoke, not with reason, for a long time, until half the night was gone. Only then did she withdraw with her woman into another room and leave him in her own chamber with a little boy to wait on him in case he lacked something.

It was a hot night, and so as soon as Andreuccio found himself alone he stripped down to his vest and took his trousers off and laid them out at the head of the bed. As soon as he had done this, nature called him to empty his great bulging stomach. He asked the boy where he could do this and was directed to a door in the corner of the room. "Go in there," the boy said. He went through the door confidently and found his feet were on a wooden plank which had broken loose from the joist at the opposite end. The plank flew up, and man and wood tumbled down. His guardian angel protected him, however, and although he fell from a great height he didn't hurt himself. Instead, he covered himself in the stinking filth the place was full of. So you may get a clearer picture of the place, I will describe it to you. This was a narrow alley such as you often see between houses. A pair of rafters stretched between the houses. To these, various boards had been attached and a place for relief set up. It was one of these boards that had given way with Andreuccio.

Finding himself at the bottom of the alley and greatly distressed by the accident, he started shouting for the boy. The latter, however, as soon as he had heard him fall, ran straight to his mistress. She lost no time in running to his chamber, where she located his clothes and found the money. Her trick had worked, and now that she had what she wanted she couldn't care less about him, and immediately shut the door through which he had gone.

Andreuccio received no reply from the boy and shouted even more loudly, but to no avail. Seeing this, his suspicions were aroused and he began to smell a fox. He then scrambled over a low wall that shut the alley off from the street. He let himself down into the road, went up to the door of the house, which he recognized only too well, and beat on it and shouted loudly for a long time. But this was all in vain. He moaned and groaned and fully realized the nature of his unlucky accident.

"Heaven help me," he cried, "how could I lose five hundred florins and a sister in such a short space of time!" He yelled and screamed and shouted all kinds of things and started once more to hammer at the door. He did this for so long and with such vigor that he woke up the neighbors who wouldn't tolerate this din. One of these, a waiting woman of the courtesan, came to the window, supposedly all bleary-eyed, and said tartly:

"Who's down there knocking?"

"What?" cried Andreuccio. "Don't you recognize me. It's Andreuccio, Madam Fiordaliso's brother."

To this she replied:

"My good man, you've obviously drunk too much. Go and sleep it off and come back tomorrow morning. I don't know any Andreuccio nor any of these tales you're telling. Off you go quietly and let us sleep, if you don't mind."

"What?" replied Andreuccio. "You don't know what I'm talking about? I know you do, but if this is what Sicilian relationships are all about then at least return my clothes and I'll willingly clear off."

"My good man," she countered, as if laughing, "you must be dreaming."

Without more ado she withdrew her head and shut the window. This fully confirmed Andreuccio's loss. His despair turned to anger and then to madness. He decided to use violence where words had failed. He picked up an enormous stone and began battering at the door more furiously than ever.

Now many of the neighbors who had been woken up and left their beds thought he was some malicious fellow who had trumped up this story to spite the woman of the house. They were provoked by this repeated knocking and came to their windows and ganged up on him like a pack of dogs.

"What a crying shame to come to a decent woman's house at this time of night with these cock-and-bull stories. For God's sake, man, get away from here and let us sleep. If you have some business with her, come back tomorrow and spare us this noise tonight."

The gentlewoman's henchman took comfort in these words and came to the window of the house. Andreuccio hadn't seen or heard of this man before. He spoke in a rough coarse voice:

"Who is down there?"

Andreuccio, hearing this, looked up at the window and made out the powerful figure of a man with a bushy black beard on his face. He was yawning and rubbing his eyes as though he'd just been woken from a deep sleep.

Not without some fear, Andreuccio answered:

"I am the brother of the lady of the house."

The other didn't wait for him to finish but said, more fiercely than before:

"I don't know why I don't come down there and beat your brains in. You must be a drunken jackass to keep us awake like this."

Then he drew back into the house and shut the window. Some of the neighbors, who were well acquainted with this man's character, cautiously advised Andreuccio:

"For God's sake, man, leave quietly and don't stay there to be killed. For your own good, get away from there."

Andreuccio, terrified by the man's voice and looks, and moved by the neighbors' pleas, which seemed to stem from goodwill, set off for his inn. He went in the direction the maid had led him previously, but he really didn't know which way to go. He grieved for his money and was the saddest man alive. He was repulsive to himself because he stunk so foully, and thought he might go down to the sea to wash. He turned to the left and followed a street called Riga Catalana, which led to the upper part of the city. Immediately he saw two men coming toward him with a lantern, and fearing that they might be officers of the watch or the like, he crept into a hovel that was close by. They, however, as though with evil intent, made straight for the same place. They entered, and one of them took an iron lever from his shoulder, which they examined while chatting to each other.

It wasn't long before one of them said:

"What is it? I can smell the worst stench ever." So saying, he raised his lantern and, seeing the wretched Andreuccio, asked with amazement:

"Who is there?"

Andreuccio didn't say anything, so they went up to him with the light and asked him what he was doing there in such a mess. He told them everything that had happened to him, and they, guessing where this all took place, said to each other:

"That would have been at Scarbone Buttafuoco's house." Then they turned to him and one said:

"My good man, even though you've lost your money you still have good reason to praise God that this accident happened and you couldn't get back into the house again. If you hadn't fallen, rest assured that once you were asleep you would have been knocked on the head and lost your life as well as your money. What good does it do to be sad? You're as likely to catch a falling star as get any of your money back. Worse than that, you'd probably get yourself killed if you made a fuss about it."

Then they spoke together for a while and said to him:

"Listen, we feel sorry for you, so if you're prepared to throw in with us, you're sure to get a larger share than what you lost."

When Andreuccio heard this he declared he was ready.

Now that day an archbishop by the name of Messer Filippo Minutolo had been interred in his finest robes and with a ruby on his finger that was worth more than five hundred florins. They told Andreuccio of their plan to rob the archbishop. Andreuccio, out of greed, followed them to the cathedral. As they walked one of the thieves said:

"Can't we find somewhere for this man to wash? It doesn't matter where just so long as he doesn't stink like that."

"Yes, we'd better," the other answered. "We're close to a well where there used to be a rope and pulley and a huge bucket. Let's go there and he'll soon be clean."

So saying, they went to the well and found the rope, but the bucket had been removed. They decided to tie him to the rope and lower him into the well so that he might wash. They told him to give the rope a pull as soon as he was clean and they would haul him up.

They had hardly let him down when, as luck would have it, certain officers of the watch, thirsty from the heat and from chasing after some villain or other, came up to the well for a drink. When the two rogues saw them they became agitated and ran off before they themselves could be seen. When Andreuccio, at the bottom of the well, had washed himself, he pulled on the rope. The thirsty officers, putting down their targets, arms, and greatcoats, began to haul on the rope, thinking the bucket at the other end was full of water. As soon as Andreuccio found himself near the top, he let go of the rope and grasped the rim with both hands. When the officers saw this, they started back in fear, dropped the rope, and without a word took to their heels as fast as possible. Andreuccio was astonished and, if he hadn't held on to the rim, would have certainly fallen to the bottom and injured or killed himself. However, he managed to clamber out and, finding the arms, which he knew didn't belong to his companions, was even more astonished. He didn't know what to make of it but, suspecting further treachery, he determined to hurry on without touching anything. Thus he went on his uncertain way, grumbling about his bad luck.

As he left he met his two companions, who had come back to pull him out of the well. When they saw him they too were amazed and asked who had hauled him out. Andreuccio replied that he didn't know and told them exactly what had happened and what he had found next to the well. The others, realizing what had happened, laughed, and told him why they had fled and who had pulled him out. Then, because it was the middle of the night, they stopped talking and went straight to the cathedral, which they entered quietly. Once inside, they went up to the enormous tomb of the archbishop. The lid was very heavy, and they raised it with their iron levers and propped it open wide enough for a man to enter. This done, one of them said:

"Who's going in?"

"Not me," the other replied.

"And not me either," the other said. "Let Andreuccio go in."

"No, I won't go in," the latter said.

When the two rogues heard this they said:

"What! You won't? If you don't get in there we'll beat you to death with one of these levers."

Andreuccio became afraid and crept into the tomb. He thought to himself:

"These fellows want me inside so that they can cheat me. When I've given them everything they'll take off and leave me struggling to get out of the tomb. I'll be left empty-handed." With this in mind, he determined to make sure he got his share first. As soon as he got to the bottom, he remembered the ring they'd been discussing previously. He pulled it off the archbishop's finger and put it on his own. Then he passed them the crozier, mitre, and gloves and stripped the man down to his shirt and gave them everything. He told them there was nothing else there. The others declared that the ring must be there and told him to look all over the place. Andreuccio said he couldn't find it and made a great show of looking, which kept them guessing for some time. Finally the two rogues, who were no less cunning than he was, told him to have a really good look. Then they took away the lever that had been holding up the lid and made off, leaving him shut up in the tomb.

You may well imagine what became of Andreuccio when he found himself in this sorry state. He tried again and again to budge the lid with his head and shoulders, but only succeeded in tiring himself out. Overcome with sorrow and despair, he fainted on top of the archbishop's corpse. Whoever saw him there wouldn't have been able to tell who was deader, the prelate or Andreuccio. He soon came round, however, and burst into a flood of tears. He realized he was destined for one of two ends. If no one came to the tomb, he would die of hunger and rot among the worms of the dead body; on the other hand, if someone came and found him there, he would certainly be hanged as a thief.

In this dejected frame of mind he heard people stirring and talking inside the church, and soon realized that they were there for the same reason he and his comrades had come. Fear redoubled its grip on him. The newcomers forced open the lid of the tomb and propped it up. Then they started arguing about who should go in. No one volunteered. However, after a long dispute, a priest said:

"What are you afraid of? Do you think he's going to eat you? The dead don't eat men. I'll go in myself."

So saying, he stuck his chest against the rim of the tomb, and with his face turned out, lowered his legs down. When Andreuccio saw this, he grabbed the priest by his legs and made a show of offering to pull him down into the tomb. The priest let out a terrible cry and flung himself out of the tomb. As for the others, they fled in terror as though pursued by a hundred thousand devils. The tomb was left open.

When Andreuccio saw this he was filled with happiness and swiftly scrambled out of the tomb and went out of the church the same way he'd come in. It was nearly daylight as he went on his way with the ring on his finger. At last he came to the seashore, and from there he made his way back to the inn, where he found his comrades and his host, who'd been worrying about him all night long. He told them everything that had happened to him, and they all agreed with the host that it would be best if he left Naples. Thus it was that he went back to Perugia, having invested his money in a ring when he really came to buy horses.

# Fra Puccio's Penance

*A ribald, light-hearted spoof of unnatural and exaggerated piety,*
*Boccaccio's tale reflects medieval literature's tendency to satirize*
*religious hypocrisy and ambition.*

ear San Pancrazio there lived an honest rich man whose name was Puccio di Rinieri. In his later years this man gave himself up almost entirely to religious practices, became a lay brother of the the order of Saint Francis, and was known as Fra Puccio. He lived a devout life and went to church often. He had no family except for his wife and a maid. It wasn't in his disposition to apply himself to a trade. Being an ignorant clodhopper, he said his Paternosters, went to sermons, attended mass, and never failed to be present whenever praises were chanted. He fasted, mortified himself, and, it was rumored, even scourged himself.

His wife, whose name was Mistress Isabetta, was still a young woman of twenty-eight to thirty or thereabouts. She was fair, fresh, and buxom as an apple. Because of the piety and age of her husband, she kept longer and more frequent fasts than she really liked. When she felt like sleeping or having pleasure with him, he responded by telling her about the sermons of Fra Nastagio or the Complaint of Mary Magdalene or some such thing. At this time, a monk called Sir Felice, related to the order of San Pancrazio, returned home from Paris. This monk was young, quick-witted, and a profound scholar. Fra Puccio and he became great friends. On account of this, Sir

Felice resolved all his doubts and, knowing his pious turn of mind, made him a show of much devoutness. Fra Puccio, for his part, brought him home for dinner or supper when the occasion offered. The lady, likewise, for her husband's sake, grew acquainted with him and paid her respects.

The monk continued to visit Fra Puccio's house and, seeing how fresh and plump the wife was, guessed what thing it was that she most lacked. He decided therefore, if he could, to supply her needs in the shape of himself and thus spare Fra Puccio any weariness. Thus, craftily catching her eye at one time and another, he sought to light in her breast that same desire that burned within his. When he saw it, he told her of his wishes at the first opportunity. But though he found her like-minded in this enterprise, he could find no way of bringing it to fruition, for she wouldn't trust herself to be with him anywhere else in the world except her own house, where such a thing was impossible because Fra Puccio never left town. This caused the monk a great deal of sorrow, but after considering the matter he hit upon a scheme whereby he might keep company with the lady in the house without drawing suspicion, even though Fra Puccio was at home. Accordingly, the latter coming one day to visit him, he spoke in these terms:

"I have often understood, Fra Puccio, that your greatest desire is to become a saint, but it seems to me you are taking the longest route. There is another, a very short one, which the pope and the other great prelates, who know and practice it, will not have  publicized. This is because the clergy, who live mostly by alms, would be put out, inasmuch as the laity would no longer trouble themselves to support them with alms and the like. However, as you are my friend and because you have honorably entertained me, I will teach it to you if you will practice it and not tell it to another living soul."

Fra Puccio, eager to know this thing, at once begged him to instruct him in this. He swore he would never tell it to anyone and, if it were possible, follow the teaching.

When the monk heard this, he said:

"Since you have promised, I will tell you. You must know that the learned men of the Church believe that whoever performs this penance should be blessed, but understand me, I am not saying that after the penance you will not be a sinner as you are now. However, the sins which you have committed up to the time of the penance will by virtue of it be purged, and you will be pardoned. Those sins which you commit afterward will not be written against you but will pass away with the holy water, as happens with venial sins now. In the first place, then, a man must when he begins a penance confess his sins with the utmost diligence. After this he must fast for forty days, and during this time he must abstain from touching women — even his own wife. In addition, you must have a place in your house where you can see the sky at night. You must go there at nine o'clock and set up a wide plank in such a way that it stands upright and you can lean your loins against it, keeping your feet on the ground, and stretch your arms out, crucifix fashion. If you wish to rest them on some peg or other, you may. In this way you must remain gazing up at the sky without moving a muscle till matins. If you were a scholar you would do well to repeat certain prayers I could give you, but as you are not, you must say three hundred Paternosters and the same number of Ave Marias in honor of the Trinity. Looking up at heaven, keep in mind that God is the creator of heaven and earth and remember the passion of Christ, who hung on the cross in a similar way. When the bell sounds matins, you may, if you wish, dressed as you are, go to your bed and sleep. Afterward, in the forenoon, take yourself to church and there hear at least three masses and repeat fifty Paternosters and the same number of Ave Marias. After this, with firm purpose in your heart, you may do whatever you have to do and dine. At evensong, however, be in church again, and there offer up certain prayers which I will write out for you and without which nothing is achieved. Then toward nine o'clock return to the already mentioned state. If you do this, as I have done myself in the past, I have no doubts that before you come to the end of the penance, you will (provided you have performed it with devotion and compunction) experience the majesty of eternal love."

Fra Puccio said:

"This is not a very burdensome matter nor that long, and it may well be done. In God's name, I intend to begin on Sunday."

He then took leave of his friend, returned home, and told everything in its proper order to his wife, as the other had said he might. The lady understood only too well what the monk meant by having him stand fast without moving until matins. The scheme appeared excellent to her. She replied that she was well pleased with it and with every other good work that he did for the health of his soul, and so that God might make the penance profitable to him, she would even fast with him, but not more than that. Thus they reached an agreement.

Sunday came, and Fra Puccio began his penance. The lordly monk, having made arrangements with the lady, came most evenings to sup with her. He brought with him a store of good things to eat and drink, and afterwards he lay with her till matin song. Then he got up and took himself off whilst Fra Puccio returned to bed.

As it happened, the place where Fra Puccio had chosen for his penance was next to the chamber where the lady lay. There was only a thin wall between them. One night when our master monk made overfree with his lust and she with it, it seemed to Fra Puccio that he felt the floor of the house shaking. Having at this time said a hundred of his Paternosters, he made a stop there and without moving called out to his wife and asked her what she was doing. The lady, who had a sense of humor and was then like a rider of San Benedetto's beast or that of San Giovanni Gualberto, answered:

"To tell you the truth, husband, I am tossing because I have to."

"What?" said Fra Puccio, "you're tossing? What do you mean, tossing?"

The lady laughed, for she was a playful woman and doubtless had reason to laugh. She answered merrily:

"What? You do not know what it means? I have heard you say it a thousand times: 'Who suppeth not by night must toss till morning light.'"

Fra Puccio did not doubt that the fasting was the cause of her inability to sleep and that was why she tossed about the bed. Therefore, he spoke simply from the heart:

"Wife, I told you not to fast, but since you do, try to forget about it and get some sleep. You are vaulting about the bed so much it is making everyone shake."

"Do not concern yourself with it," answered the lady. "I know what I am doing. You do well, and I will do as well as I can."

So Fra Puccio held his peace and once more addressed himself to his Paternosters. After that night, however, my lord monk and his lady made a bed in another part of the house, where they stayed in utmost joy for as long as Fra Puccio's penance lasted. Then at one and the same time the monk took his leave and the lady returned to her own bed, where a little while later Fra Puccio came from his penance. In this way the latter continued to do his penance while his wife took her delight with the monk. She often used to say merrily to him:

"You have Fra Puccio performing a penance which has brought us Paradise."

Indeed, the lady was in fine fettle and took such a liking to the monk's fare, having for so long been on her husband's low diet, that when Fra Puccio's penance was accomplished, she still found means to eat her fill with him elsewhere. Discreetly, she long took her pleasure with him.

Thus then, so my last words match my first, it happened that whereas Fra Puccio thought to win Paradise for himself, in fact he won it for the monk. The latter had shown him the swiftest route. As for his wife, who lived with him in direst need, Sir Felice, like the charitable monk he was, guaranteed her all she needed.

# The Lustful Monk

*A bawdy, irreverent satire on medieval religious institutions, this tale from Boccaccio's* Decameron, *playfully explores the hypocrisy of self-righteousness.*

n Lunigiana, a country not far from here, there was once a monastery more blessed with monks than it is today. One of these monks was young, vigorous, and lewd, and no amount of fasting and vigil could assuage his lust. One day, toward noon when all the other monks were sleeping, this monk took a stroll around the convent, which stood in a very solitary place. Here he happened to catch sight of a very well endowed girl, probably the daughter of a local husbandman. She was gathering herbs from the fields. No sooner had he set eyes on her than he was violently stricken by carnal appetite. With this in mind, he started a conversation with her. One thing led to another and, unseen by any, she agreed to accompany him to his cell. There, carried away by too much ardor, he took pleasure with her less cautiously than was prudent. It so happened that the abbot had just got up and was walking quietly past the monk's cell when he heard the racket the two of them were making. He went stealthily up to the door so that he might better recognize the voices. At once it became obvious there was a woman in the cell, and at first he thought to throw open the door on them. However, on reflection, he decided on another course of action, returned to his chamber, and waited for the monk to emerge.

The monk, although taken up with the wench, his great pleasure and his delight in her company, was nevertheless on his guard. He thought he heard some scuffling of feet in the dormitory and, setting his eye to a peephole, clearly made out the abbot listening to him. Then he realized only too well that the latter had got wind of the wench's presence in his cell. He knew this would result in sore punishment, and fell into a fit of melancholy. However, without telling his troubles to the girl, he turned matters over in himself to find a means of escape. He soon struck up a fine ruse which would serve him well. Thus, pretending he had tarried long enough with the girl, he told her:

"I must go and find out how you can get out of here without being seen. Stay here quietly until I return."

Then he went out, locked the cell door behind him, and betook himself straight to the abbot's chamber, where he presented him with the key, as was the custom when monks went abroad. With an innocent face, he said:

"Sir, I was unable to finish bringing back all the wood I chopped this morning, so with your permission I will go immediately to the wood and bring back the rest."

The abbot, assuming he hadn't been seen by the monk, was glad of such an opportunity to discover more fully the nature of the offense. Accordingly, he took the key and granted the monk the permission he sought. As soon as the monk had gone, the abbot considered the best course of action. He could open the cell in the presence of all the other monks, so that they could see the misdeed and wouldn't murmur against him when he punished the offender; or he could learn from the girl what had happened. It occurred to him that she might be the wife or daughter of a local man and that therefore he shouldn't shame her in front of all the monks. He then made up his mind to see her first and reach a decision. Thus, he went to the cell, opened it, entered, and shut the door behind him.

When the girl saw the abbot enter she was full of dread for fear of being shamed, and burst out crying. The lord abbot, however, saw that she was young and comely. Old as he was, he suddenly felt the pricks of the flesh as keenly as his young monk had. He said to himself, "With all this stress and trouble around me, why don't I take some pleasure when I have a mind? This is a handsome wench and nobody knows she's here. If I can have my way with her, why shouldn't I? Who will know? No one will know, and a sin that's hidden is half forgiven. Maybe I'll never get a chance like this again. It makes sense to avail ourselves of good when the Almighty provides it."

Having reasoned with himself in this way, he changed his previous plans and sat down beside the girl. Gently he began to comfort her. He begged her not to weep. He moved from one sentence to another, and ended up telling her of his desire. The girl, who was neither hardhearted nor stubborn, agreed readily enough to give the abbot his pleasure. The latter, after he had held her tightly and kissed her again and again, got up onto the monk's pallet. Having equal regard for the grave burden of his dignity, the girl's tender age, and his great weight, he did not lie on her breast but sat her upon him and took pleasure with her thus for a long time.

Meanwhile, the monk, who had only pretended to go to the wood, had hidden himself in the dormitory. When he saw the abbot enter his cell alone he was reassured. He had no doubts that his ruse would work, and when he saw the door locked from within he was quite certain. He came out of his hiding place and crept to the peephole, through which he heard and saw all that the abbot said and did.

When it seemed to the abbot that he had stayed long enough with the girl, he locked her in the cell and returned to his own chamber, where, after a while he heard the monk stirring and guessed he had returned from the wood. He thought he would rebuke him severely and throw him into prison so that he alone might possess the fair prey. Accordingly, he sent for him, and with a grave face ordered that he should be put in prison.

The monk answered readily enough:

"Sir, I have not yet been with the order of Saint Benedict long enough to know all its ways. You had not yet shown me that monks should make women a means of mortification, as with fasts and vigils. Now you have shown me, however. I promise you, with your forgiveness, never to offend again, but only to do as I have seen you do."

The abbot, who was a quick-witted man, immediately realized that the monk not only knew more than he did but had actually seen what he had done. Then his conscience pricked him for his own default and he was ashamed to inflict on the monk a punishment which he equally merited. He therefore pardoned him, charging him to keep silent about what he had seen, and secretly they led the girl out. And rumor has it that she returned to that cell more than once.

# Melusina

*Sorcery and demonology were omnipresent concepts in the medieval mind, and Melusina, at once nurturer and enchantress, combines in a single persona the witch and the mother. The legend is anonymous.*

mmerick, count of Poitou, was a nobleman of great wealth and eminent virtues. He had two children, a son named Bertram and a daughter Blaniferte. In the great forest that stretched in all directions around the knoll on which stood the town and castle of Poictiers lived a Count de la Forêt, related to Emmerick but poor and with a large family. Out of compassion for his kinsman, the Count of Poitou adopted his youngest son, Raymond, a beautiful and amiable youth, and made him his constant companion in hall and in the chase.

One day the count and his retinue hunted a boar in the forest of Colombiers, and, outdistancing his servants, Emmerick found himself alone in the depths of the wood with Raymond. The boar had escaped. Night came on, and the two huntsmen lost their way. They succeeded in lighting a fire, and were warming themselves over the blaze when suddenly the boar plunged out of the forest upon the count. Raymond snatched a sword and struck at the beast, but the blow glanced off and slew the count. A second blow laid the boar at his side. Raymond then perceived with horror that his friend and master was dead. In despair he mounted his horse and fled, not knowing where he went.

Presently the boughs of the trees became less interlaced and the trunks fewer, and, the next moment, his horse crashed through the thicket and brought him out on a pleasant glade, white with rime and illumined by the full moon. In the midst of the glade bubbled a limpid fountain that flowed with a soothing murmur, away over a pebbly floor. Near the fountain-head sat three maidens in glimmering white dresses, with long wavy golden hair and faces of inexpressible beauty.

Raymond was riveted to the spot with astonishment. He believed that he saw a vision of angels, and would have prostrated himself at their feet had not one of them advanced and stayed him. The lady inquired as to the cause of his terror, and the young man, after a slight hesitation, told her of his dreadful misfortune. She listened with attention, and at the conclusion of the story recommended him to remount his horse, gallop out of the forest and return to Poictiers as though unconscious of what had taken place. All the huntsmen had lost themselves in the wood that day, and were returning singly at intervals to the castle, so no suspicion would attach to him. The body of the count would be found, and from the proximity of the dead boar it would be concluded that he had fallen before the tusk of the animal to which he had given its death blow.

Relieved of his anxiety, Raymond was able to devote his attention exclusively to the beauty of the lady who addressed him, and found means to prolong the conversation till daybreak. He had never beheld charms equal to hers, and the heart of the youth was completely captivated by the fair mystery. Before he left her he obtained from her a promise to be his. She then told him to ask of his kinsman Bertram, as a gift, as much ground around the fountain where they had met as could be covered by a stag's hide. Upon this ground he would undertake the building of a magnificent palace. Her name, she told him, was Melusina, she was a water fairy, of great power and wealth, and she consented to be his, but on one condition: that her Saturdays might be spent in a complete seclusion that he should never venture to intrude upon.

Raymond then left her and followed her advice to the letter. Bertram, who succeeded his father, readily granted the land Raymond asked for, but he became slightly vexed when he found that by cutting the hide into threads, Raymond had succeeded in making it cover a considerable area.

Raymond then invited the young count to his wedding, and the marriage festivities took place with unusual splendor in the magnificent castle erected by Melusina. On the evening of the marriage the bride, with tears in her eyes, once again implored her husband on no account to attempt an intrusion on her privacy on Saturdays, for such an intrusion must infallibly separate them forever. Raymond swore to observe her wishes strictly.

Melusina continued to extend the castle and strengthen its fortifications, till the like was not seen in all the country.

In the course of time the Lady of Lusignan gave birth to a son who was baptized Urian. He was a strangely shaped child; his mouth was large; his ears pendulous. One of his eyes was red, the other green. A twelvemonth later she gave birth to another son whom she called Gedes, who had a face that was scarlet. In an offering of thanks for his birth she erected and endowed the convent of Malliers, and as a place of residence for her child built the strong castle of Favent.

Melusina then bore a third son, who was christened Gyot. He was a fine, handsome child, but one of his eyes was higher up on his face than the other. For him his mother built La Rochelle. Her next son, Anthony, had long claws on his fingers and was covered with hair. The next child had but a single eye. The sixth was Geoffrey the Tooth, so called from a boar's tusk which protruded from his jaw. She had other children, all in some way disfigured and monstrous.

Years passed, and the love of Raymond for his beautiful wife never diminished. Every Saturday she left him and spent twenty-four hours in the strictest seclusion, without her husband ever thinking of intruding on her privacy. The children grew up to be great heroes and illustrious warriors. One, Freimund, entered the Church and became a pious monk in the abbey of Malliers. The aged Count de la Forêt and the brothers of Raymond shared in his good fortune, and the old man spent his last years in the castle with his son, whilst the brothers were furnished with money and servants suitable to their rank.

One Saturday the old father inquired at dinner after his daughter-in-law. Raymond replied that she was not visible on Saturdays. Thereupon one of his brothers, drawing him aside, whispered that strange gossiping tales about this Sabbath seclusion were circulating, and that it behooved him to inquire into it and set the minds of the people at rest. Full of wrath and anxiety, the count rushed off to the private apartments of the countess, but found them empty. One door alone was locked, and that opened into a bath. He looked through the key-hole and to his dismay beheld her in the water, her lower extremities changed into the tail of a monstrous fish or serpent.

Silently he withdrew. No word of what he had seen passed his lips. It was not loathing that filled his heart, but anguish at the thought that by his fault he must lose his beautiful wife who had been the charm and glory of his life. Some time passed by, however, and Melusina gave no token of consciousness that she had been observed during the period of her transformation. But one day news reached the castle that Geoffrey the Tooth had attacked the monastery of Malliers and burned it, and that in the flames had perished Freimund with the abbot and a hundred monks. On hearing of this disaster, the poor father, in a paroxysm of misery, exclaimed as Melusina approached to comfort him: "Away, odious serpent, contaminator of my honorable race!"

At these words she fainted, and Raymond, full of sorrow for having spoken thus intemperately, strove to revive her. When she came to herself again, with streaming tears she kissed and embraced him for the last time. "O husband!" she said tenderly, "I leave two little ones in the cradle. Look tenderly after them, bereft of their mother. And now farewell for ever! Yet know that thou, and those who succeed thee, shall see me hover over this fair castle of Lusignan whenever a new lord is to come." And with a long wail of agony she leapt from the window, leaving the impression of her foot on the last stone it touched.

The children in arms she had left were Dietrich and Raymond. At night the nurses beheld a glimmering figure appear near the cradle of the babes, most like the vanished countess, but from her waist downwards terminating in a scaly fishtail enameled blue and white. At her approach the little ones extended their arms and smiled, and she took them to her breast and suckled them. But as the gray dawn stole in at the casement she vanished, and the children's cries told the nurses that their mother was gone.

Long after this it was still believed, in France, that the sad figure of Melusina would appear over the ramparts of her castle, Lusignan, before the death of any one of its lords; and that after the passing of her family, she was to be seen whenever a king of France was about to die.

# Fra Cipolla

*This is the ninth story of the sixth day in Boccaccio's* Decameron. *Like many of Boccaccio's tales, it is a good natured satire of the hypocritical clergy and the commerce of the church.*

ertaldo, as you may know, is a burg of Val d'Elsa situated in our country, which, small though it be, was once inhabited by gentlemen and men of substance. It was in this town that one of the friars of the order of Saint Anthony long used to visit once a year, to reap the alms bestowed by the simple peasants. His name was Fra Cipolla. This Fra Cipolla was a little person, red-haired and merry of countenance, the jolliest rascal in the world, and, though he was no scholar, he was so fine a talker and so ready of wit that those who did not know him would not only have esteemed him a great rhetorician, but had avouched him to be Tully himself or maybe Quintilian. He was gossip, friend or well-wisher to well nigh everyone in the country.

One August he betook himself thither according to his habit, and on a Sunday morning, when all the goodmen and goodwives of the villages around had come to hear mass at the parish church, he came forward and said, "Gentlemen and ladies, it is, as you know, your usance to send every year to the poor of our lord, Baron Saint Anthony, some of your corn and oats, this little and that much, each according to his means and his devoutness, to the intent that the blessed Saint Anthony may keep watch over your beeves and asses and swine and sheep. Besides this,  you are required to pay that small tithe which is due once a year. To collect these I have been sent by my superior, to wit, my lord abbot. Now, with the blessing of God, you may leave the church when mass is over, but late this afternoon, when you hear the bells ring, return here where I will preach to you after the wonted fashion and you shall kiss the cross. What is more, for that I know you all to be great devotees of our lord Saint Anthony, I will, as a special favor, show you a very holy and goodly relic, which I myself brought from the holy lands beyond seas: one of the Angel Gabriel's feathers, which remained in the Virgin Mary's chamber, when he came to her in Nazareth." This said, he broke off and went on with his mass.

Now, when he said this, there were in the church two roguish young fellows, one Giovanni del Bragoniera and the other Biagio Pizzini, who, after laughing with one another awhile over their friend Fra Cipolla's relic, plotted together to play him some trick in the matter of this holy feather. Accordingly, having learned that he was to dine that morning with a friend of his in the town, as soon as they knew him to be at table, they took themselves to the inn where he had alighted, purposing that Biagio should hold his servant in conversation, whilst Giovanni should search his baggage for the feather, whatever it might be, carry it off, and wait to see what he should say to the people of the matter.

Fra Cipolla's servant, called Guccio Balena, was such a scurvy knave that his master used oftentimes to jest of him and say, "My servant hath in him nine faults, such that, were any one of them in Solomon or Aristotle or Seneca, it would suffice to mar all their worth, all their wit and all their sanctity. Consider, then, what a man he must be, who hath all nine of them and in whom there is neither worth nor wit nor sanctity." Being questioned as to what these nine faults were, and having put them into doggerel rhyme, he would answer, "I will tell you. He's a liar, a sloven, a slugabed; disobedient, neglectful, ill bred; o'erweening, foul-spoken, a dunderhead; besides which he has sundry other pecadilloes, of which it is better not to speak. But what is most laughable of all his manners is that, wherever he goes, he is still for taking a wife and hiring a house; for, having a big black greasy beard, he sees himself as so exceedingly handsome and agreeable that he believes all the women who see him fall in love with him. If you let him alone, he would run after them all till he collapsed. Suffice it to say, he is of great assistance to me, for that none can ever seek to speak with me secretly without his hearing his share; and if it chance that I be questioned about anything, he is so fearful, lest I should not know how to answer, that he straightaway answers for me, either Yea or Nay, as he judgeth suitable."

Now Fra Cipolla, in leaving his servant at the inn, had bidden him to take care that none touched his gear, and most particularly his saddlebags, for that was where the sacred things were. But Guccio—who was fonder of a kitchen than the nightingale of the green boughs, especially if he scented some serving-wench, had seen at the inn a gross fat cookmaid, undersized and ill-made, with a pair of paps like manure-baskets and the face of a beggar, all sweaty, greasy and smoky—left Fra Cipolla's chamber and all his gear to care for themselves and swooped down upon the kitchen, as the vulture swoops upon carrion, and seated himself by the fire. For all that it was August. He entered into the wooing of this scullery maid, who was called Nuta, telling her that he was a gentleman in his own right, with an estate of more than nine-million florins, after that which he gave to others, making it out to be rather more than less. This was, of course, all stated without regard to his hat, which was coated with enough grease to season a stockpot, or his doublet, all torn and pieced and enameled with filth about the collar and under the arms, with more spots and patches of divers colors than ever had Turkey or India cloth, or his shoes, all broken with hose unsewn. He told her that he meant to clothe her and trick her out anew and deliver her from the wretchedness of working for others, and bring her to hope of better fortune, and many other things, which, for all his earnest delivery, was of course just hot air and would come to nothing, as did all of his enterprises.

The two young men, accordingly, found Guccio busy about Nuta, and were well pleased, as it spared them half their pains. They entered Fra Cipolla's chamber, which they found open. The first thing that came under their inspection were the saddlebags. In these they found, enveloped in a great taffeta wrapper, a little casket, and opening this discovered a parrot's tail feather, which they concluded must be that which the friar had promised to show the people of Certaldo. And, in truth, he might easily cause it to be believed in those days, for the refinements of Egypt had not yet made their way into our land, save a small part of Tuscany, as they have since done in very great abundance, to the undoing of all Italy. The rude honesty of the ancients yet endured in Certaldo; not only had the people never set eyes on a parrot, but were far from having even heard tell of such a bird. The young men, rejoicing at finding the feather, laid hands on it, and, not to leave the casket empty, filled it with some coals they saw in a corner of the room. Then, putting all things in order as they had found them, they made off in high glee with the feather, without having been seen, and began to await what Fra Cipolla should say, when he found the coals.

The simple men and women who were in the church, hearing that they were to see the Angel Gabriel's feather that afternoon, returned home as soon as mass was over, and, neighbor telling it to neighbor and gossip to gossip, no sooner had they all dined than so many men and women flocked to the town that it would scarce hold them, all eager to see the relic. Fra Cipolla, having dined well and slept awhile, arose a little after three and hearing of the great multitude of country folk come to see the feather, sent word for Guccio to come thither with the bells and bring his saddlebags. Guccio, tearing himself with difficulty away from the kitchen and the lovely Nuta, took himself with the things required to the church door and fell to ringing the bells lustily.

When all the people were assembled there, Fra Cipolla, not observing that aught of his had been meddled with, began his preaching and said many words about his adventures; after which, thinking to come to the showing of the Angel Gabriel's feather, he first recited the Confiteor with the utmost solemnity and lit a pair of candles. He delicately unfolded the taffeta wrapping and brought out the casket. Having first pronounced certain ejaculations in praise and commendation of the Angel Gabriel and his relic, he opened the casket and seeing it full of coals, suspected not Guccio of having played him this trick, for he knew him not to be man enough; nor did he curse him for having kept ill watch, but silently cursed himself for having committed to him the care of his gear, knowing him to be negligent, disobedient, careless and forgetful.

Nevertheless, without changing color, he raised his eyes and hands to heaven and said, so as to be heard by all, "O God, praised be thy might!"

Then, shutting the casket and turning to the people, "Gentlemen and ladies, you must know that, while I was yet very young, I was dispatched by my superior to the east, and it was expressly commanded me that I should seek till I found the Privileges of Porcellana, which, though they cost nothing to seal, are much more useful to others than to us. On this errand I set out from Venice and passed through Borgo de' Greci, whence, riding through the kingdom of Algarve and Baldacca, I came to Parione, and from there, not without thirst, I came after a while into Sardinia. But what boots it to set out to you in detail all the lands explored by me? Passing the Straits of San Giorgio, I came into Sillya and Trikkya, countries much inhabited and with great populations, and thence into the land of Falsia, where I found great plenty of our brethren and friars of other religious orders, who all went about those parts, shunning discomfort for the love of God, heeding little of others' pain and toil, and spending no other money than that which is uncoined. Thence I passed into the land of the Abruzzi, where the men and women go in clogs over the mountains, and a little farther I found folk who carried bread on sticks and wine in bags. From this I came to the Mountains of the Bachi, where all the waters run downhill; and in brief, I made my way so far inward that I was at last to India Pastinaca, where I swear to you, by the habit I wear on my back, that I saw a great merchant, cracking walnuts and selling the shells retail.

"Being unable to find that which I went seeking, for from there one can go on only by water, I turned back and arrived in those holy countries where, in summer-years, cold bread is worth four farthings a loaf and the hot is given for nothing. There I found the venerable father my lord Blamemenot Anit-pleaseyou, the very worshipful patriarch of Jerusalem, who, for reverence of the habit I have still worn of my lord Baron Saint Anthony, would have me sell all the holy relics that he had about him and which were so many that, were I to recount them all to you, I should not come to an end for several miles. However, to please you, I will tell you about some of them. First, he showed me the finger of the Holy Ghost, as whole and sound as ever it was, and the forelock of the seraph that appeared to Saint Francis and one of the nails of the Cherubim and one of the ribs of Christ himself and some of the vestments of the Holy Catholic Faith and sundry rays of the star that appeared to the Three Wise Men and a vial of the sweat of Saint Michael, from when he fought with the devil, and the jawbone of the death of Saint Lazarus and others.

"And in return for that I made him a free gift of the Steeps of Monte Morello in the vernacular and of some chapters of the Caprezio, which he had long gone seeking. He made me a sharer in his holy relics and gave me one of the teeth of the Holy Rood and a little of the sound of the bells of Solomon's Temple, in a vial, and the feather of the Angel Gabriel; and he gave me also the coals with which the most blessed martyr Saint Lawrence was roasted. All of these things I devoutly brought home with me and yet have. It is true that my superior has never allowed me to show them until such a time as he should be convinced if they were true or not. But now, by certain miracles performed by them and by letters received from the patriarch, he has been made certain of this, and has granted me leave to show them; and I, fearing to trust them to others, still carry them with me.

"Now I carry the Angel Gabriel's feather, so it may not be marred, in one casket, and the coals with which Saint Lawrence was roasted in another, the two being so like one to other that it has often happened that I have taken one for the other. This is what has passed this day, for, thinking to bring with me the casket with the feather, I have brought that which has the coals. I do not hold this to have been an error; nay, it seems to me certain that it was God's will, and that he himself placed the casket with the coals in my hands, especially now I mind me that the feast of Saint Lawrence is but two days hence. It is clear that God, knowing that, by showing you the coals with which the Saint was roasted, wanting me to rekindle in your hearts the devotion you should have for him, caused me to take not the feather but the blessed coals extinguished by the sweat of that most holy body. So, my blessed children, put off your bonnets and draw near devoutly to behold them; but first I would have you know that whosoever is marked by these coals, in the form of the sign of the cross, may rest assured, for the whole year to come, that fire shall not touch him without his feeling it."

Having thus spoken, he opened the casket, chanting a canticle in praise of Saint Lawrence, and showed the coals. After the simple multitude had beheld them awhile with reverent admiration, they all crowded about Fra

Cipolla, and making him better offerings than they usually did, begged him to touch them with the relics. Accordingly, taking the coals in hand, he fell to making the biggest crosses he could find room for upon their white smocks and doublets and upon the veils of the women, telling them that however much the coals dimished in making these crosses, they grew again afterwards in the casket, as he had proven many a time. In this way he crossed all the people of Certaldo, to no small profit, and, by his ready wit and presence of mind, baffled those who had thought to baffle him by taking the feather. These two, Giovanni and Biagio, being present and hearing the rare shift employed by him and how far he had taken it and with what words, had laughed so that they thought they would crack their jaws. After the common folk had departed, they went up to him and, with all the mirth in the world, confided to him what they had done and returned his feather to him, which next year stood him in as good stead as the coals had done that day.

# The Priest and the Blackberries

*An exemplary didactic tale with an ironic twist, this moralistic narrative attacks hypocrisy with hilarity.*

 certain priest, having need to go to the market, called for his mare to be saddled and brought to the door. The mare had carried her master for over two years, and was as sleek and well fed as he was, having never known hunger or thirst, or lack of sweet hay and oats. The priest climbed into the saddle and set out on his journey. I know the month was September, for it was the season when blackberries grow upon the bushes in great plenty and abundance. The priest rode toward the town repeating his hours, his matins and his vigils.

Approaching the gate to the town, the path ran through a grove, and raising his eyes from his book, the priest spied a bush thick with blackberries, plumper, darker, and more ripe than any he had ever seen. Desire entered his heart, for overly covetous was he of this fair fruit, and, slowly checking the pace of his mare, he brought her to stand next to the richest bush.

Yet one thing still came between him and his desire. The blackberries near the ground were surrounded by spines and sharp thorns, whilst the sweetest and plumpest fruit grew so high up on the tree that in no way could he reach them from the saddle. The priest pondered for some time. After a while his desire overcame his fear, and he slowly climbed up and stood with his feet on the saddle. Once there, by leaning over just a little, he could pluck the fruit. He chose the fairest, the ripest and the sweetest bunches, devouring them as swiftly and greedily as he could pick them. The good mare beneath him moved not an inch, but patiently awaited her master's bidding. Now, when this priest had eaten his full of the blackberries, he looked down and saw that the mare was still standing calm and gentle beneath him, with her head toward the back of the thicket. The priest was well pleased with himself and his mare, for he had safely eaten his full and his feet were still steady on the saddle of the mare, who was very tall. "Good Lord!" thought he, "would that anyone should call out 'Gee-up!'" But he spoke the words at the same time as he thought them, and the mare, frightened, bolted forward, tumbling the hapless priest into the thicket where the thorns and briars grew the thickest and sharpest. There he was left, in that inhospitable bower, and not for a king's ransom could he move an inch, neither backward nor forward, without doing even more harm to his already scratched and bleeding person.

The mare galloped straight back to her stable and, seeing her return without a rider, the priest's household were greatly alarmed. They cursed the mare for being an evil and unfaithful nag, and the housekeeper swooned dead away, convinced her master was lost. After they had gathered their wits about them a little, they proceeded to run to and fro in the fields and lanes, calling for the priest. At length they came down the path near where their master lay in his shame and misery. On hearing their sad calls for him, he raised his voice in a piteous cry; "O my friends, do not pass me by, for this couch of thorns is an uneasy bed: it is my blood that stains these thorns berry red!"

The servants followed the sound of his voice and found the priest. "Father," they cried, "who has done this to you?"

"Alas," he replied, "it is the sin of gluttony that made me fall. This morning as I rode by here reciting my hours, I saw and smelled the perfume of this fruit, and overreaching myself was cast down into these thorns. But help me out, for now all I wish for is to return home, see the surgeon, and rest from my wounds."

The lesson of this short tale is clear: It is not always wise to say out loud what you think to yourself.

# Suggested Reading

## TEXTS

*Andreas Capellanus: The Art of Courtly Love*, trans. John J. Parry (New York: Columbia U. P., 1941; abr. F. Lock, New York: Ungar [M-104], n.d.).

*The Works of Geoffrey Chaucer*, ed. F.N. Robinson (Boston: Houghton Mifflin, 1961).

*Parsival*, by Wolfram von Eschenbach, trans. A.T. Hatto (Harmondsworth, England: Penguin Books, 1980).

*Confessio Amantis*, John Gower, abr. and trans. Terence Tiller (Baltimore: Penguin Books [L128], 1963).

*Fabliaux: Ribald Tales from the Old French*, trans. Robert Hellman and Richard O'Gorman (New York: Thomas Y. Crowell, 1965).

*The Romance of the Rose*, by Guillaume de Lorris and Jean de Meun, trans. Harry W. Robbins (New York: E.P. Dutton, 1962).

*The Portable Medieval Reader*, eds. James B. Ross and Mary M. McLaughlin (New York: Viking Press, 1949).

*Tristan*, by Gottfried von Strassburg, trans. A.T. Hatto (Harmondsworth, England: Penguin Books, 1960).

*Arthurian Romances*, by Chretien de Troyes, trans. W.W. Comfort (London: Everyman's Library, 1913).

*The Golden Legend of Jacobus de Voragine*, trans. Granger Ryan and Helmut Ripperger (New York: Longmans, Green and Co., 1941).

*The Bestiary: A Book of Beasts* , T.H. White, (New York: G.P. Putnam's Sons [Capricorn Books, 26], 1960).

## STUDIES:

Henry Adams, *Mont-Saint-Michel and Chartres* (Boston: Houghton Mifflin Co., 1905).

Norman F. Cantor, ed. *Medieval World: 300-1300* (New York: MacMillan, 1978).

Ernst Curtius, *European Literature and the Latin Middle Ages* (New York: Harper and Row [Harper Torchbooks, TB2015], 1963).

John Huizinga, *The Waning of the Middle Ages* (Garden City, N.Y.: Doubleday [Anchor Books, A42], 1954).

W.T.H. Jackson, *Medieval Literature: A History and a Guide* (New York: Collier Books, 1966).

C.S. Lewis, *The Discarded Image: An Introduction to Medieval and Renaissance Literature* (Cambridge: The University Press, 1967).

Roger Sherman Loomis, *The Development of Arthurian Romance* (New York: Harper and Row [Harper Torchbooks, TB1167], 1964).

Barbara W. Tuchman, *A Distant Mirror: The Calamitous Fourteenth Century* (New York: Knopf, 1978).

Jessie L. Weston, *From Ritual to Romance* (Garden City, N.Y.: Doubleday [Anchor Books, A125], 1957).

# Acknowledgments

We would like to thank the many museums, libraries, archives, firms, photographers and individuals below who supplied or granted permission to reproduce the illustrations in this book. Every effort has been made to trace and procure permission from the primary sources and the producers wish to apologize if in any case the acknowledgements made below are inadequate. In no case is any such inadequacy intentional and if any owner of copyright who has not been located contacts the producers, a reasonable fee will be paid and required acknowledgements made in future editions of this book.

JACKET FRONT   Ms. Cod. Marc. Lat. I, 99 f. 8v Biblioteca Nazionale
                Marciana, Venice
JACKET BACK   National Gallery, London
PLATES
33   Wilton Diptych, National Gallery, London
34   Ms. Fr. 3479 f.550 Bibliothèque Arsenal, Paris
51   Ms. 9243 f.45, 1468 Bibliothèque Royale Albert 1°, Brussels
52   Musée de Cluny, Paris
69   Ms. Add. Meladius 12228 f. 202v. British Library Board
70   Ms. Royal 14 E111 f.89 British Library Board
87   Cod. 2617, fol. 53 Österreische Nationalbibliothek, Vienna
88   Ms. Cod Marc. Lat. I, 99f. 8v Biblioteca Nazionale Marciana, Venice
105   Ms. Cotton Nero AX f. 94 British Library Board
106   Ms. Amb. 317. 2f. 10r Stadtbibliothek, Nuremberg
123   Ms. Fr. 112 f.5.C. Bibliothèque Nationale, Paris
124   Ms. Douce 383 f.16 Bodleian Library
157   ARS. 5070 fol. 27 Bibliothèque Nationale, Paris
158   Ms. Add. 27695 f.14r British Library Board
175   ARS. 5070 fol. 54v° Bibliothèque Nationale, Paris
176   Metropolitan Museum, New York